# THE BOOK BOOK

*'That man is in the book business,*
*that man is a publisher.'*

Ben Sonnenberg pointing out
Alfred Knopf at a party
(story told by Alastair Cooke)

*by the same author*

non-fiction

THE PUBLISHING GAME

fiction

FAMILY BUSINESS

Dick Lyon

# THE BOOK BOOK

Anthony Blond

Anthony Blond

JONATHAN CAPE
THIRTY-TWO BEDFORD SQUARE LONDON

29.09.03

First published in 1985

Reprinted 1985

Jonathan Cape Ltd,
32 Bedford Square, London WC1B 3EL

British Library Cataloguing in Publication Data

Blond, Anthony
The book book.
1. Publishers and publishing. – Great Britain
I. Title
338.4'70705'0941 Z323

ISBN 0–224–02074–9

Photoset in Great Britain by
Rowland Phototypesetting Ltd, Bury St Edmunds, Suffolk
and printed by St Edmundsbury Press,
Bury St Edmunds, Suffolk

To Messrs C. Hoare & Co.

# *Contents*

# *Preface*

In *The Mighty Micro*, published in hardback by Gollancz at £6.95, with two impressions, and in paperback by Coronet at £1.95, the late Christopher Evans, who died young, explains how and why the book will be supplanted by, amongst other technological breakthroughs, the microchip. The information, instruction and even the delight the reader once obtained from books will soon be supplied by other shinier, trickier, fiddlier and doubtless sexier-looking artefacts. As one contemplates a photograph of Christopher Evans in his booklined study, one wonders what led him to this conclusion.

Every invention in communication from radio to television, from video to word processor, has signalled the doom of the book, but since the advent of television in the United States, book sales there have increased fourteenfold.

Design an artefact which is frequently original, non-pollutant, biodegradable, portable, silent, easily reproducible, information-retrievable, cheap, imperishable, translatable, accessible, aesthetically appealing, financially appreciable (the last two not invariable), and the answer is the book.

Moreover, I hope to show that, far from becoming outmoded, it is remarkably resilient and adaptable.

*Note*
Of the 21,000 in the publishing game no section circulates more vivaciously than the editors and publicists; consequently

some of their designations may be out of date. However, if they change their jobs they keep their style, and few drop out.

A.B.

# Acknowledgments

*The Book Book* has been through many hands for checking and suggestions; none of those involved is responsible for the opinions expressed.

There are so many facts that a few must be wrong.

I'm sorry.

I must particularly thank Sarah Toynbee for her research and Joan Forbes for her typing, Venetia Pollock who made sense of a turgid manuscript and who bullied me without ruth but with charm, and Graham C. Greene, of Jonathan Cape, for his overlordly encouragement.

For permissions, interviews and contributions thanks are due to the following: John Beer, Eric de Bellaigue, *The Bookseller*, Melvyn Bragg, Doug Bristow, John Brown, Uli Bruno, Carmen Callil, Ian Chapman, Anthony Cheetham, Isabel Colegate, Robin Denniston, Toby Eady, Marilyn Edwards, Faber & Faber, Bryan Forbes, Martyn Goff, Peter Grose, Bruce Harris, Philip Howard, Walter Jeffrey, Terence Kilmartin, Roger Kirkpatrick, Philip Larkin, Robert MacDonald, Dr Peter Mann, Tom Maschler, Sonny Mehta, Timothy Mo, James Morton, Peter Owen, Dieter Pevsner, John Prime, *Publishers Weekly*, *Punch*, Harold Robbins, Deborah Rogers, Bernice Rubens, Michael Sissons, Society of Authors, *The Spectator*, Nicholas Spenceley, Peter Stern, David Taylor, *The Times*, Ion Trewin, Ed Victor, Lord Weidenfeld, Fay Weldon, A. N. Wilson, and Simon Wratten.

A.B.

# I *Authors*

In olden times the storyteller was outside society, he wandered like a gypsy, telling tales, rarely his own, of the deeds of gods and heroes. It has always been important to spread abroad what men thought of the gods, and gods thought of men, and such information formed much of the content of early incunabula. When the printing press came into use, the propaganda value of this new invention was quickly recognized by the Church, who wished to reserve its use for their theologians; its immediate power was exemplified by William Tyndale, whose translation of the Bible was the first British bestseller. He made the Scriptures intelligible so that every farmhouse in England had a copy. Too intelligible for the Establishment: Henry VIII complained that the Bible was being quoted like 'jingles' in the alehouses of the City of London. The radical element in Jesus's teaching was recognized as dangerous; Tyndale's Bible was suppressed and its author, through the efforts of the Bishop of London, was strangled, then burnt at the stake at Vilvorde near Antwerp in 1536. His version is still not available: some enterprising publisher should reissue it, though they may not have a bestseller on their hands today. Bibles, contrary to what one might think, are not always good business, they come in too many editions. The Jewish Lords Weidenfeld and Sieff joined with Oxford University Press to bring out a cheap Bible on India paper for sale only in Marks & Spencer at £4.99, but it was not a fast mover.

Tyndale understood that to sell well, to make an impact, a book must have something specific to say, be clear, concise and easily available; it helps too if the message contains ideas people already want to hear. The Authorized Version, which has prevailed for so long, was deliberately Latinized, designed to be declaimed from the lectern, not thumbed through over the kitchen table. 'Sufficient unto the day is the evil thereof,' says the A.V. 'Each day has its share of troubles,' says Tyndale. Different but . . . intelligible.

As a profession, writing has always been precarious. Authors have suffered for their pains in every era. Some have died of broken hearts, neglect and poverty like Chatterton, others have not been acclaimed in their own time, like Mervyn Peake or Henry Green, but rehabilitated safely dead. John Keats was another victim – massacred by the *Edinburgh Review:*

> 'Who killed John Keats?'
> 'I' said the Quarterly
> Savage and tartarly
> 'I killed John Keats!'

Yet others have been frowned upon by society for indulging in an unmanly, unladylike, certainly ungentlemanly, occupation. There is no mention on Jane Austen's tablet in Winchester Cathedral that she ever wrote a book. The writer has usually been underpaid and the world has thought it right that this should be so: cherished occasionally, but never to excess.

The arrival of the literary agent, the 1911 Copyright Act and the activity of the late John Gould's Writers' Guild, the glittering prizes of film, television deals and paperback auctions, have changed the climate. Now *some* authors can make serious money. The quality of writing which pushes earnings up into six figures may not have eternal value and may have induced what is referred to elsewhere in this book as blockbuster pathology among publishers, but it has focused attention on the media's need, indeed craving, for talent. Many films are based on ideas gleaned from books. The average writer may earn less than the usual wage of a house painter but the author's working life is viewed as agreeable and there is always the possibility, lurking over the horizon, that the next bestseller will be his.

Writers in the English language possess an edge over their colleagues in Greenland or Gabon, even though successive governments have not considered that writing belongs to the arts. Despite the introduction of Writers in Residence by the Arts Council and Regional Arts Associations and the increase in bursaries and literary prizes, the profession is poorly favoured by the public purse. Even the successful campaign by the Writers' Action Group to gain extra royalties for authors much thumbed in public libraries, which resulted in the Public Lending Right bill, seems to help only the popular few. However, the first year's crop from PLR helped to fill the pockets and certainly the hearts of some well-circulated authors. Alan Williams, who had not written a novel for several years, got a cheque for £3,000. Despite all the vicissitudes, people continue to write.

There are those who scribble away in the evenings and at weekends, blanketed from everybody except the muse, in every spare moment. Others type full-time, which for a writer is three or four hours of creative composition a day: the continuous art of creation is so exhausting that more would merely mean worse. Oblivious, incapable of social intercourse, a bugbear to wives, husbands, lovers, children, the writer ploughs a lone furrow whilst all around him, or her, friends and family grow jealous of the whole enterprise unless they are utterly devoted.

Ideal surroundings are those where the telephone, newspapers and (for some) a mirror are absent, places which are square, boring, certainly unromantic and preferably anonymous. Trachtenberg conceived his mathematical thesis in Auschwitz, but it is better to choose an establishment which offers regular meals. Harold Robbins secludes himself in a suite in a Manhattan hotel, Jean Genet has been a full-board resident in a small hotel in Kifissia, Snetterton (his *petit ami* of the day was a racing driver), Passy or Montreal. A prison cell or a cabin without a porthole on a boat full of bores, if provided with that most inspiring of all prospects, a blank paper, are all a writer needs to write. The process is not agreeable, but it has been said that there is only one thing worse than writing and that is not writing.

Some rare birds invent out of their own imagination; others act first, climbing mountains, sailing seas or crossing deserts, and then write about it all afterwards, gritting their teeth as they grapple with the pen; camels, spars and jumars being so much easier to master. There are those who research from the library, hunting around for a good subject, delving into letters, anecdotes and personalities in order to marshal all into an elegant biography; the Victorians have recently proved an excellent field for study. Some subjects seem never to fail; Royalty, the Mountbatten family, Churchilliana continually please the public. There are others whose autobiographies are also instant bestsellers on the names alone, never mind the content: Nureyev, Olivier, Niven; the vision of these people in the public eye is so lovable that motes are ignored.

A great many authors are commissioned by publishers to cover some apparent gap on the library shelf. More than one third of Jonathan Cape's annual non-fiction list consists of books which the publishers have paid for in advance and have asked specifically to be written for them. Commissioning an author is fraught with peril but the constant quest for new ideas makes publishers always willing to take the risk. Sometimes the author is thought of first, maybe a title or even a name; the book is then built around a concept.

For example, Vivienne Knight, alias Lady Glenavy, was asked by Trevor Howard to write a warts-and-all biography of him. She thought the perfect title for the life of this cricketer, jazz musician, actor and film star, who had been married to the same woman for forty years, would be *A Gentleman and a Player*. She then rang me up. Delighted with the idea, I telephoned my favourite bookshop to test sales potential. 'Smaller than Olivier but bigger than John Mills,' was the verdict. As publishers hope to recover their advance payments not only through hardback sales but through paperback editions, American rights, and serials in newspapers – in that order – I telephoned next a paperback house for their reaction. 'Big,' they replied, which I took to mean that they might eventually offer £10,000 to £15,000 for the finished product. Jotting down the costs on the back of an envelope I worked out that if the book were to sell 10,000 copies in hardback, if the manuscript were to be about 80,000 words long with 32 pages of photographs, which would be expensive, but after all the man is a film star, then it might be priced at around £12.50. We might therefore be able to clear our costs and pay the author an advance of about £7,500 plus expenses. So I commissioned her to go ahead and she buzzed off to Sri Lanka to research Trevor's childhood.

A great many publishers make these kinds of calculations all the time, with variations, because so many authors are commissioned, including novelists. It is of course easier for the managing director of a small firm to make quick decisions on the telephone than it is for the chairman of a giant corporation, but even the large publishers dream up books out of their heads. Occasionally some public event or newspaper article triggers off the same idea simultaneously in several publishing brains, which accounts for two or three books coming out at the same time on a subject which has previously remained untouched. Other subjects seem to be left alone, there are few books on moral rearmament or on chastity.

Writers are sometimes approached and asked if they would turn out a bestseller with the help of the publishing house's editor. 'The firm needs a blockbuster,' the editor cries, 'I've got to have a biggy.' And then the editor looks for a name known to the public, offers in-house energy and manufactures the book to suit the market. Mike Korda of Simon & Schuster: 'We need two a season, otherwise we're dead.' Paperback publishers with a slot empty will consciously overpay for a lead title.

I was in Corfu one year, with just enough local wine inside me to provide inspiration, when I remembered a visit I'd made to Glyndebourne to hear Richard Strauss. It occurred to me that no one had written about the social side of the Nazi party. Strauss's opera had first been performed in Munich in 1943. What had the first night been like?

On my return to England I commissioned the novelist

Gillian Freeman, married to the Nazi buff Edward Thorpe. For her researcher she chose one of Hitler's Aryan babies who lived with a Jewish ballet dancer in Knightsbridge. The book was about one Elisabeth von Schwarzenberger, and Alan Clark, the military historian, wrote that 'it gave a more valuable insight into the ethos of the Nazi party than many a more learned tome'. Unfortunately the author, in an interview with Valerie Jenkins of the *Evening Standard*, blew the story as an invention. The American publisher tried to back out of his contract, but so powerful was the creation that I was telephoned by tearful readers wanting to believe that the heroine was alive and well and living in Florida. This experience of faking enabled me to know, immediately I heard that Rupert Murdoch's News International had bought *Hitler's Diaries*, that they were fakes.

Some writers do not produce just the odd imaginative fantasy but churn them out to order several times a year. They often use different names. Mills & Boon, who had the distinction, if that is the word, of being the only imprint known and referred to by the great British public when ordering rather than referring to title or author, commission each of their writers to produce two or three romantic novels a year to a set pattern.

The romantic novel brigade are a formidable band – mostly women, often wealthy, occasionally heads of Oxford women's colleges. All too often their works are imagined to be bland, in the image of Barbara Cartland, Denise Robins or Georgette Heyer, but medieval life gives many of them a chance to describe murder, rape, pillage, hanging and quartering with no holds barred. Costume, too, plays a great part in such books, particularly in the works of Mary Renault (pseudonym for Mary Challans), who lived in a sensational house at Camps Bay, Cape Town; sitting there, gazing out of the window, watching the surf riders trying to break their legs, one could actually smell the spray and the salt. Frequently hard-hitting, controversial and uncompromising, she usually wrote about those endeavouring to come to terms with their homosexuality. Her bestsellers about Alexander the Great, *Fire from Heaven* and *The Persian Boy*, were salaciously elegant, challenging the orthodox historian, but she was a born storyteller even if her work has been described as 'upper-class buggery'.

There is a whole publishing manufactory centred round the Bloomsbury Group. The Mitfords, self-pollinated, bloom annually. Maybe it is time to call a halt. The Pakenham clan's industry *is* the book business. Prolific and profuse, they are headed by Frank, Earl of Longford, who is a director of the publishers Sidgwick & Jackson (which is financed by Lord Forte, a former waiter detained in 1940 as an Italian under Regulation 18B; a former owner of Sidgwick & Jackson, the late Jim Knapp-Fisher, lent £1,500 to Carlo's wife during the war to help her run her milk bar, hence the connection). Lord Longford is famous for his championship of doubtful causes and his sense of publicity – one of his five books is surprisingly entitled *Humility*. His wife Elizabeth has written five historical books, two on Wellington; his nephew Ferdy Mount is literary editor of the *Spectator* and has written *The Subversive Family*. His eldest sister, Mary Clive, has written *Christmas with the Savages*; another sister, Violet Powell, has written three books; she is married to Anthony Powell, who has written a series of novels called *Dance to the Music of Time*, reckoned to be among the ten best in the English language. His son, Thomas Pakenham, has written about the Boer War; his daughter Rachel Billington has written four novels and is possibly the highest rated in the literary stakes in the clan, whilst the best known to the general public is his daughter Antonia Fraser (now married to Harold Pinter) who has turned out a dozen books, notably *Cromwell, Our Chief of Men*, a life of Mary Queen of Scots and a series of detective stories. Another Pakenham daughter, Judith Kazantzis, is a poet.

Whodunits, beginning with Edgar Allan Poe, gained popularity with Wilkie Collins's *The Moonstone* and peaked with Sherlock Holmes, of whom Conan Doyle had a surfeit – 'like too much *pâté de foie gras*'. In between the wars, the writers of these stories developed their own set of rules, making them popular with dons, politicians and clergymen. Peter Dickinson kept to the three unities for his first two books, both Golden

Dagger Award winners, just to make writing them more enjoyable.

Such writers are probably looked down upon by what one might call the PEN club lot, Iris Murdoch, A. N. Wilson, John Fowles, Caroline Blackwood and both Naipauls, all of whom are in the High Lit. game, contestants for the Booker Prize, always happy to sign letters to *The Times* demanding the release of their Polish colleagues. (The accretion to their ranks of serious prose has given what was once a somewhat etiolate society a pleasing rush of blood to the head.)

There are writers who begin just by trying to pass the time. Angus Wilson (né Frank Johnstone) spent endless hours as Deputy Superintendent of the Reading Room at the British Museum watching eccentric scribblers frenetically researching. Amused by what he saw, he produced two crisp volumes of short stories, *Wrong Set* and *Such Darling Dodos*. Gradually he developed his short stories into novels; slowly books took over his career, he became a university teacher, was knighted for his worldwide crusade on behalf of the British Council and, as the Grand Old Man of English Literature, has had his novel *Old Men at the Zoo* serialized on BBC television.

Books can indeed take over a man's life. Simon Raven received his first break reviewing in the *Listener* when it was edited by J. R. Ackerley of *My Dog Tulip* fame. Hugh (now Lord) Thomas suggested to me that I commission Simon to write a novel, so I drew up a contract which stipulated that he live more than a hundred miles from London and receive fifteen pounds a week. Whereupon Simon sat down and produced the whole *Alms and Oblivion* series around his hero Fielding Gray, who was fired from his public school (for 'a cloud no bigger than a boy's hand'), fired from his Cambridge college and fired from the army. Inevitably Simon's friends and contemporaries suspected that these novels were mildly autobiographical and looked at the characters to see whom they recognized. James Prior might have imagined he was the inspiration for Peter Morrison; I was amused to think I had something to do with the Jewish publisher Gregory Stern, but Hugh Thomas was most upset to be associated with the picture of Tom Llewellyn and made no bones about it.

When Hugh Thomas suggested I commission Simon, he himself had just edited – we are back in 1958 – a volume of essays called *The Establishment* (not, interestingly, listed in his *Who's Who* entry), which was an attack on various English institutions like the Civil Service by Thomas (late Lord) Balogh, on the public schools by John (late Lord) Vaizey and others. The attacks were perceptibly from the left, from which position the editor and contributors have now profitably diverged. Like so many intellectuals Hugh had left the Foreign Office over Suez, and had written a novel called *The World's Game* about the horrors of unemployment in high positions if the disarmament talks at Geneva were ever to succeed. He was himself currently unemployed and spent the afternoons glazedly watching films in Shaftesbury Avenue while looking in the evenings for a safe Labour seat. In this predicament he did not care for his affinity with Tom Llewellyn. To avoid the possibility of a libel action, Simon subsequently drew a rather better profile for Tom: he got his own television programme, was elected to a Cambridge college, married brilliantly and climbed even higher.

Not even Raven could have predicted that Hugh Thomas himself would become a professor, *the* authority on Spanish Affairs, and now, as Margaret Thatcher's 'history goy' (I am indebted to another of her advisers for this apt if esoteric description), the Chairman of Policy Studies in Downing Street. Nor probably did Simon see himself becoming an established, prolific, steam engine of a writer, gaining his main income from such television successes as *Edward VIII & Mrs Simpson*, the Palliser series and from doctoring film scripts. He has been described as one of the most underrated writers in England, a veritable modern Trollope.

But all the people I have mentioned so far are established writers: what is it like to try and try and try to get published? To find out I asked David Taylor, who was born in Norfolk in 1960. Here is the authentic voice of a typical English potential author, middle-class, slightly overeducated, lacking experience but not ambition:

'There were no outlets for creative writing at school, though from time to time local poets were hauled in to listen to the compositions of a sixth-form literary society. "I think," Anthony Thwaite once remarked, actually wincing as he did so, "that this was a poem you *had* to write." After that I confined myself to lapidary editorials in the school magazine. "Brevity, as Horace observes, goes hand in glove with obscurity," ran the first sentence of one of them. The manuscripts of the fantasy novels stayed in the drawer along with the polite letter from Allen & Unwin explaining that "Tolkien was already well-established in this field." It seems to me that I was utterly talentless.

Next came Oxford, where everybody wanted to write. In fact you could hardly throw a stone without hitting somebody engaged upon the Oxford novel that would knock *Zuleika Dobson* into a cocked hat or the spiky Donneish poetry then being made fashionable by Craig Raine. It was possible for anybody with a little ingenuity to get published practically anywhere. I wrote a fortnightly column for the Oxford equivalent of *Private Eye*, the odd political piece for *Cherwell*, short stories (of a mildly pornographic nature) for the *Isis*. I do not think that anybody took much notice of them.

The first payment I ever received for a piece of literary work was a Postal Order for £1 for a poem published in *Outposts* when I was twenty. Rather than encouraging me this signalled the end of any poetic aspirations. I never wrote another poem. Short stories sent to *The London Magazine*, *Encounter* and so on invariably come back. Yet out of the blue came a favourable sign. I can still remember the feeling of exaltation – an actual visceral stab – upon opening a copy of the *Spectator* in the Oxford W. H. Smith and finding myself listed among the contributors. Two days later arrived a cheque for £60. A week later, having left it on the mantelpiece for people to admire, I banked it.

Leaving Oxford with no job and few prospects it seemed reasonable to mine this particular lode. I applied to Alexander Chancellor for a commission, was sent to write an article about Liverpool, and received an even larger cheque.

Paradoxically, unemployment was a marketable commodity. Newspapers, I discovered, were crying out for pieces written by "Graduates on the Dole". The *Daily Telegraph* took one of mine. Eventually I did get a job and the need to write these pieces receded. But you only have to receive a single sum of money for a piece of writing to acquire a taste for it. I despatched articles with an urgency that suggested they were a fresh instalment of the scriptures, haunted literary agencies like a ghoul, took on any hack-work that presented itself: booksellers' catalogues, queer ghost-writing jobs for obscure publishers, half a book for Guinness Superlatives. If I have any opinions about the fate of "young writers" they are largely favourable. As a general rule, I should say, most editors do read what is sent to them and consider it objectively, although thoughts of back-scratching do haunt undergraduates sick of the sight of self-addressed brown paper envelopes and letters beginning "Dear X. I regret . . ."

But what about the money? Almost the first question asked in England of anyone who announces that he or she is a writer, "Yes – but can you make a living out of it?" Quite obviously I cannot; and I suppose that only a twentieth of people describing themselves as "authors" actually do. A look at the arithmetic (my arithmetic) will demonstrate how difficult it is.

To support yourself in London, even in standards of average comfort, you need a minimum of £6,000 a year. This sounds a lot – and it will be pointed out that Faulkner wrote his first novel lying on a coke heap – but it does not include all the accessories of popular imagining, mistresses, wine cellars and so forth. No, £6,000 a year will just about suffice to feed you, clothe you, pay your rent and buy you the odd book, without whose stimulus you will never write anything at all.

Now, at the time of writing (December 1983) I earn, approximately, £10,000 a year. Three-quarters of this comes in the form of a monthly salary cheque, the rest can be described as 'literary earnings'. And how did I come by this? £1,000 was an advance on a book, another £500 came from occasional articles and reviews. The rest came in a variety of ways – editing jobs, reading for agents, *New Statesman* competitions. It was not easily come by, and it is not enough. If I wanted to write full-time I should have to triple (at least) this form of income.

Consequently, I cannot afford to give up my job as a copywriter in a PR agency. Not that I really want to be able to do this. Even at its most trivial level (press releases) it involves writing. Meanwhile, the business of trying to get published proceeds with painful slowness. After I came down from Oxford I wrote a short, frivolous novel about the place called *The Garden Party*: nobody would publish it. At the moment I am trying to write a long, dense novel about Norfolk (and other places) whose provisional title is *Great Eastern Land*. It is proving to be a laborious exercise. I do not know if I will ever finish it or, more important, if anyone will want to put it into print.'

David Taylor epitomizes trying: let us now look in detail at success, at the lives, style and work of two fiction writers, an archetypal American, Harold Robbins, possibly the highest-paid writer in the world and, as a complete contrast, an English country-house novelist, Isabel Colegate. They typify the extremes of the profession. All they have in common, as far as I know, is that I once published them both.

Harold Robbins must be the most consistently bestselling writer in the United States. The blurb from his recent novel *Spellbinder* (New English Library) tells the success story. 'More than 220,000,000 copies of Harold Robbins's novels have been sold around the world. His books have been translated into almost every language, making him the most widely read American novelist today.'

Born in New York on May 21st, 1916, Harold Robbins grew up in the Depression. He left school at fifteen and a half to go to work, first on the snow-removal squad, then as an errand boy, soda jerk, counterman, cashier, icecream pedlar on the beach at Coney Island, bookie's runner and then inventory clerk for a small chain of grocery stores, his success at which encouraged him to go into the food-factoring business on his own. Before he was twenty-one he had made his first fortune and lost it. He went bankrupt for over a million dollars and had to begin all over again. In 1940 he got a job as a shipping clerk in the warehouse of Universal Pictures and worked his way up to become executive director of budget and planning for the entire company. When he was thirty years old he began to write. His first novel, *Never Love a Stranger*, was written at odd moments late at night, was completed in 1947 and became an immediate bestseller. There followed in quick succession *Dream Merchants*, *Stone for Danny Fisher*, *Never Leave Me*, *79 Park Avenue* and *Stiletto*.

It was then that Robbins had to choose between his writing and his business career. For him there could only be one choice, writing. His next major work, *The Carpetbaggers*, became one of the most widely read novels ever published. He then wrote *Where Love Has Gone*; *The Adventurers*; *The Inheritors*; *The Betsy*; *The Pirate*; *Lonely Lady*; *Dreams Die First*; *Memories of Another Day*; and *Goodbye, Janette*.

I published the British and Commonwealth edition of *The Carpetbaggers* in 1963. I spell this out because it differed from the American edition in the suppression, by me one sunny weekend, of all the four-letter words and the softening of the more lurid or, as the code-name goes, 'explicit' passages, for the benefit of the then more tender British susceptibilities in general, and for those of W. H. Smith in particular. It was a great success, not just through its lubricity, but for its cliff-hanging skill and the bizarre information which it contained. Harold Robbins invented *faction*, that skilful blend of fiction and fact, which gives veracity, poignancy and verisimilitude to a book. *The Carpetbaggers*, based on the career of the late Howard Hughes, instructs the reader on how to design a brassière, fly an aeroplane and milk a film company. The story-line is so strong that I contemplated a cadet edition, as had been done successfully for Nicholas Monsarrat's *The Cruel Sea*; that is, an edition with all sex removed, making it suitable for children and their school libraries.

The hardback, though it sold 200,000 copies, was but the stalking horse for the launch of the paperback edition by the

New English Library (then a subsidiary of the Times/Mirror group, now an imprint of Hodder & Stoughton), when Gareth Powell, legendary Welsh lorry driver turned impresario, imported the author for a promotional tour. He was installed in the Ritz, but found it too poky and moved to the Oliver Messel suite at the Dorchester, where I brunched with him over a smoked salmon omelette prepared by his own chef. He is a pyknic, bright-eyed Jew, fierce and charming in startling terms, egotistic, energetic, generous and, as de Gaulle said of the Israeli nation, 'sur de lui'. When flying into Bristol, he noticed the pilot had gone green; he took over the controls and landed the plane.

I published two more of Harold's books, both pieces of cake, but not quite as scrumptious as *The Carpetbaggers*, and once, drinking champagne on the terrace of his large Edwardian villa in Le Cannet, I asked him what the formula was. On the back of an envelope he wrote: MONEY

POWER
VIOLENCE
SEX
MONEY ETC:

Isabel Colegate belongs to a strain of lady novelists distinct and distinguished in a particularly English way. They are as recognizably excellent as, say, the appearance of Ralph Richardson or Sir John Gielgud in a Hollywood movie. Ivy Compton-Burnett, Elizabeth Bowen, Barbara Pym, Elizabeth Taylor, Caroline Blackwood and Elizabeth Jane Howard share gentle birth, sharp eyes, impeccable diction, social coolness and a distaste for cheap effects and gratuitous violence. Isabel Colegate has a more mischievous sense of plot than, say, Ivy Compton-Burnett, where the action is limited to the arrival in the drawing room of the butler bearing a telegram on a silver tray. Despite a secluded childhood – hours spent gazing out on to the Solent from the top of her father's house on the Isle of Wight – Isabel's first novel, *The Blackmailer*, which I published in 1958 as my first book, was a powerful, imaginative work and without the self-indulgent autobiographical passages which mar so many early literary efforts.

Since then she has written and published nine novels; all but the first three, which are currently being reissued by Blond & Briggs, refer to periods before the author's own. Two are set in 1913, a trilogy concerns itself with the period between 1930 and 1956, and another chronicles the ups and downs of a Utopian community between the 1920s and the 1970s. This nosing back into the earlier years of the century in search of hints or derivations was begun by reading in her father's library, much of which is now transferred to her own in the Gothick folly near Bath where she works, surrounded by her family.

Between 1958, when I published her first novel, and 1980, when Hamish Hamilton produced *The Shooting Party*, her earnings from writing had been negligible, few of her novels selling more than 2,000 copies in hardback. However, this last work, an elegant and powerful tale concerning a weekend party in a large Edwardian country house on the eve of the First World War, won the W. H. Smith literary award. *The Shooting Party* was an excellent book in its own right and was immediately recognized by her publishers as being outstanding. Christopher Sinclair-Stevenson gave it a very good jacket, plenty of advance publicity and started the buzz going around the trade: bookshops, reviewers and others were alerted. As a result it sold over 6,500 copies in hardback, and a further 8,000 copies to the Book Club. Isabel Colegate's publishers feel that it would have sold 5,000 on its merits alone judging by the excellent reviews it received: they feel that the W. H. Smith Award probably only gave it a lift of 1,500 or so copies. Be that as it may, the prize helped the author to gain wider acclaim, to sell the book well to Penguin and to America, it gave her a chance to be read by new audiences whom she had not reached before and maybe it helped to sell the film rights, for which she was paid £30,000. (The tax on this can be spread over three years, a reasonable enough provision considering that the book and the research took that amount of time to create.)

*The Shooting Party* has been filmed with Dorothy Tutin, Gayle Hunnicutt, Edward Fox, Sir John Gielgud (a delicious cameo, no doubt), Robert Hardy and Paul Scofield, who unfortunately broke his leg while shooting (the film) and had to be replaced by James Mason. It was his last film.

The enthusiasm engendered by W. H. Smith prize, film and Penguin have enabled Isabel Colegate's original publishers (me) to reissue her first three novels in one volume which has been sold to Penguin for paperback and to Viking and Avon in America. This process, the income split happily fifty-fifty between author and publisher, is known as a retread. Even so, this author's most excellent works will not compare in profitability to the least of Harold Robbins: such is the way of the world.

It is seldom realized that many, many first novels sell barely 1,000 copies in hardback and that even those authors who receive columns of space in the posh Sundays filled with encomiums may sell only a few hundred more. Paul Theroux's outstanding piece of imaginative fantasy, *Mosquito Coast*, sold only 8,000 in hardback plus 3,000 to a Book Club. Jennifer Johnston sells over 5,500 in hardback and William Boyd's *An Ice-Cream War*, runner-up for the Booker Prize, sold 15,000 copies in all.

I produce these figures so that the reader can have some idea of the huge difference between sales of the blockbuster and those of good-quality fiction, and can see why writer and publisher often quietly moan at the lack of wallet-whipping-out shown by the general public. Of course sales figures are not everything.

I was once half of the British Delegation to an International Conference of Writers at the University of Hawaii, which was L.B.J.'s present to those islands for becoming the 50th of the United States. The other – and more appropriate – half of the delegation was Malcolm Bradbury, author of *Eating People is Wrong*, *The History Man*, *Rates of Exchange*, a continual runner-up for the Booker Prize and a Professor of American Literature at the University of East Anglia.

Our theme one morning was 'the writer in society' and a bearded young American was bemoaning the writer's lot in his country. It is a cry continually heard in America at endless conferences and in the columns of the *Village Voice*. It complains that 'Publishers are in the grip of a blockbuster pathology,' that 'the middle ground in literature has been eroded by the banal,' that 'a writer's wage is less than a house-painter's at $8 an hour,' etc., etc. Oh dear!

An Indian, who we learned later had a successful electrical engineering business but was attending the conference as a poet of national repute, stood up and told us that in his country (Kerala) a writer was content with the esteem of the community. The silence was stunning.

# II *Literary agents*

Time was when all authors dealt directly with their publishers without a go-between. If publishers had all remained perfect, there would have been no need for literary agents, but some publishers have always been less perfect than others. If Thomas Chatterton had employed an agent he might not have starved to death. But there weren't any in the eighteenth century and, worse, the 'glorious boy' was not a gentleman so Horace Walpole didn't bother, despite many requests, to return his manuscript. (There were also no copying machines; *please* author person keep a copy of what you write.) Historically writers have been gentlemen, or, like Jane Austen, ladies, not dependent on the pen. Motley, a Yankee diplomat who wrote *The Rise and Fall of the Dutch Republic*, worried that his publisher might lose money on his book. Vice versa, publishers have been less concerned. Grant Richards, the publisher caricatured in Fr Rolfe's *Nicholas Crabbe*, paid Tressell £25 outright for the classic *Ragged-Trousered Philanthropists*. Publishers have been mean to authors in the past and when, in the later nineteenth century with the growth of literacy, their earnings became serious, literary agents, their shields and bucklers emerged.

If you have written a book and are too busy or too cowardly to parcel up your typescript and send it to a publisher yourself, are unsure of whom to approach, despite having read this book, and fear rejection, baffling letters or complicated legal transactions, then seek out a literary agent. He or she will scan your *magnum opus* with a friendly, experienced eye and offer knowledgeable, reasoned guidance (old friends can be over-zealous and excessively loyal). If the agent likes the book he or she may be willing to take it on: then for 10 per cent of any monies you may get, the agent will beaver away on your book's behalf.

There are over ninety literary agents mentioned in the 1984 edition of the *Writers' and Artists' Year Book* (published by A. & C. Black at £4.50) and I give my own personal selection at the end of this chapter. Do remember, when writing to any of them, to give a brief paragraph about yourself, outlining what kind of book you have written, its length overall and any other relevant information which you think will intrigue and titillate. People are much more likely to be helpful if they have some mental picture of the author or some concept of what the book is about: 'I started this novel while I was a punk down the King's Road and finished it while cleaning out tiger cages at Aspinall's zoo' will whet the appetite of the recipient, whereas a slip of paper with your name and address on it won't.

The author–publisher relationship has been likened to marriage and, like that delicate institution, it needs a broker to bring the couple together in the first place, someone to arrange the contract and to bless the union, someone, too, who will arbitrate when quarrels occur, be a guidance counsellor when life gets rough and a midwife when birth is imminent. The literary agent is marriage broker, mediator and midwife, negotiator, arbitrator and friend. With diplomatic skill a good agent will explain the intricacies of the publishing world to the author and express the hopes and fears, passions and pains of the writer to the publisher. However, the agent has to make a living out of his mart, out of being this catalyst go-between, so he will not accept a manuscript unless he thinks it is saleable. Once he has you on his list of clients, then he should promote with verve.

From the publisher's point of view, an agent can be a great asset, as sifter, sorter and source. Publishers gain many of their best authors through literary agents who save them having to trawl the oceans. They become each other's favourites: Spencer Curtis Brown helped – perhaps made – Victor Gollancz. I once met Spencer at a party and complained he never sent me any authors. 'I will,' he said, 'tomorrow; it's not great literature but it'll sell.' He was right. *Only Lovers Left Alive* by Dave Wallis was nearly filmed by the Stones and a scene from the book, when teenagers throw furniture out of the bedroom window (of my partner's house), was shown on a newsreel.

Publishers know, too, those agents who will have read the manuscript before passing it on, those who will have seen that it is at least legible, literate and suitable for their imprint. Some of the larger agents, however, are rather casual, spewing forth manuscripts in all directions, accompanied by vague letters full of errors and hyperbole: even occasionally saying 'this brilliant work of fiction', when it is biography. Honesty pays. London is small; publishers frequently meet at the Garrick, in restaurants, over dinner or at parties, so gossip soon circulates: if a manuscript has been turned down by several publishers and the agent has lied about this, or if the manuscript has been turned down by a publisher who took the author's first book, then it will quickly be known around town. An honest agent will admit that you are not the first person he has approached but that the author is willing to revise and change, or he will reduce his demands.

Agents protect publishers from neurotic and difficult authors, those who telephone all hours of the day and night, who wish to interfere in the book's production or ask ceaselessly for copies to be sent to every well-known literary name in advance for puffs. They also protect the author from having time wasted by the publisher niggling over contract imbroglios, over sales or publicity problems, so he or she can get on with writing.

Inevitably there are agents and agents: the big ones deal with the big books and will offer their mighty clients to where the money is. If they find a potential American winner, they are hardly likely to ask a tiny British publisher for a huge advance: the big agents are thus less interested in the small publisher and vice versa. But a good agent will know his markets and temper his act accordingly. Only a few knowingly represent unreliable clients who take advances from publishers with no intention of delivering a manuscript. There are, after all, also publishers who offer contracts with equivocal accompanying letters to unsuspecting young authors and then later renege on the deal. Small is often beautiful and takes more trouble: this has to be weighed against the 'muscle' of the big brokers like Ed Victor (q.v.).

Literary agents must know their foreign markets and have contacts in television and radio, film and video, and the magazine world, they should know theatrical impresarios and people who edit poetry journals, but they cannot be adept at everything so a wise author chooses an agent who specializes in the field which best applies. The small, one-man band may give you a superb lunch once in a while but he, like most agents and publishers, may have to use a foreign subsidiary, for which he may charge, to sell your work abroad. Large agencies may be able to arrange amazing auctions and bully big publishers into major publicity deals but they may also be impersonal, forgetting who you are. They should, however, have excellent specialist departments dealing daily with France and Germany, Japan and Sweden: Curtis Brown, A. D. Peters and Anthony Sheil have offices both sides of the Atlantic, on the Thames and on the Hudson, though William Morris have offices everywhere. Most London agents have their co-respondents in New York but two of the smartest, Ed Victor – who virtually commutes – and Gillon Aitken cover New York personally. (Gillon Aitken's deal for Yoko Lennon, $3.5 million sight unseen from Peter Israel of Putnam's, fell through when she backed down, but Gillon picked up a modest £18,000 for his expenses.)

Agents choose authors because they like them or their work; it is just as subjective a choice as that made by publishers, so if the first agent approached declines his help, that does not mean the manuscript is no good. All humans have their blind spots, many fail to see changes in taste or spot an original trend.

Literary agents also go hunting for new authors, perusing journals and newspapers, prowling for likely young writers with bright ideas and good subjects. They then approach these people, give them lunch, talk to them and sign them up. A simple letter of appointment will do: an agent will rarely have a contract with an author, as his right to 10 per cent of the author's proceeds is inalienable and must be paid, whether his agency is mentioned in the contract or not, always provided it can be proved that he or she sold the book in the first place. Agents spend their time at parties, in pubs, attending convivial gatherings; they listen to dinner-party conversations, remember people's names and keep their ears open for original ideas. Friends of friends can turn up trumps, as can random encounters in railway station buffets, on the grouse moor or wherever. The lone male (or female, dammit) is particularly good at sniffing the wind and scenting a potential bestseller from afar. Fast workers, they glean information and MOVE.

We asked Toby Eady, a literary agent now working in London, who spent eight years in New York, how he had found his own clients, among whom are Alex de Jongh, Christopher Hudson, Tim Jeal, Angela Fisher and Patrick Marnham.

> Clients come from recommendations, from authors who I have already made successful. Some writers will never do this but others enjoy sharing their good fortune. In the last year I have taken on eleven new clients in England, nine by recommendation by authors, three whom I approached directly: one in Africa through a personal contact in Nairobi and a television producer from Houston who came to me because he heard me lecture at a conference. As a result I have sold the works of eleven new authors in the last twelve months whilst retaining my other twenty-five. Thirty-six authors is about the number I think I can handle well.
>
> I read magazines, speak at universities, turn stones, try to look intelligently for prospective writers. I examine publishers' lists to see who is not agented, go to conferences, poetry readings, speak in public wherever writers are present and write letters to those who have written interesting articles. I ask in the first interview how much money the author wants to earn and what they have made in the past.

> I try to choose those whom I like, whose work I enjoy reading; I then know as much or as little of their personal life as seems necessary. I feel I should know what an author wants to earn and should be able to assess where they want to go; if they feel the need to change course, then I try to help. Clients do not leave you if they are happy and making a good living, if you are looking after their interests well.

Agents also get unsolicited manuscripts dropping on to the doormat. The highly efficient agency A. D. Peters, now headed by Michael Sissons, has as many authors at present as it can handle. A. D. Peters is an example of an agency well into its second generation, with a list of dead authors still contributing as well as a thriving lot of young ones coming along.

Bored by his job as a drama critic on the *Daily Chronicle*, angered by the way his writer friends were being treated by their publishers, the German-born Peters decided to start his own agency in 1924, when he was thirty-two. Soon he was helping Rebecca West, Hilaire Belloc, Evelyn and Alec Waugh and others to get better terms and to be treated with less arrogance by their publishers. His professional ethic, as his successor Michael Sissons says, was 'based on the view that an agent is an advocate, his loyalty first and last to his author'. Peters widened the role of the literary agent, branching out into backing the plays of Terence Rattigan and J. B. Priestley, producing films and associating with television companies: he helped form ATV. By furthering and enhancing his authors' causes, he became highly successful. In the words of the *Dictionary of National Biography*, he was also able to become 'a discerning collector of pictures, sculpture and furniture. He was an undercover philanthropist, who gave time and money to various causes, such as the abolition of the death penalty, a fund-raising campaign for refugee writers, and, towards the end of his life, the Arthur Koestler award for prisoners, for which he was seven years chairman of the board of trustees.'

Peters thought writers *manqués* made the best agents because they were good catalysts, but Bernice Rubens, who won the Booker Prize for *Elected Member*, published by Eyre & Spottiswoode, seems to disagree. Bernice's novel *Madame*

*Sousatzka* was made into a film in 1983; the author of eleven novels, her latest is *Brothers*. As she is one of our more successful novelists and as her peripatetic movements from house to house suggest the influence of an agent, I asked her about her relationship with her agent.

If you're a writer there will come at least one morning in your life when you wake up and want to kill your agent. This waking-thought usually occurs the day after you've handed in your latest novel. Seven hundred pages of a year's sweat and toil, to say nothing of other people's blood. Your agent's had it now for twenty-four hours, and he still hasn't phoned. You'll give him one more day, you decide. If he hasn't phoned by then you'll kill him. You get up, go to your desk and wait for the phone to ring. You won't answer it straight away. Let him wait too, the bastard. Let him, for once, be on the receiving end of indifference. When the phone does ring with some simple enquiry from an innocent friend as to the present state of your health, you curtail the conversation, panicking that your agent is phoning you meanwhile, finding you engaged and losing total interest in trying you once more. You put the phone down and curse your friend in the same breath as your agent.

You wait. Forty-eight hours pass and still no communication. On the third day you begin to wonder if your phone is out of order. You know it's working a little bit, because your neurotic waiting has been interrupted by sundry irrelevant calls. But is it working full-time? And for everybody? You dial the operator. In the thirty-five minutes it takes to get through, you reap such a harvest of sublime and universal rage, that when she finally answers, you enquire timidly whether she has yet read your novel. You hear in her voice that she pities you. She checks your number and assures you that, as far as your telephone is concerned, you are quite in order. She cannot answer for the rest of your utilities. And neither can you, because by now you are haemorrhaging with fury. You wait and you wait in vain.

On the seventh day, contrary to all biblical Law, you decide to kill your agent, and for the first time in a week, you do not spend your time waiting for the phone to ring. You spend it in salivating deliberation as to the method of his disposal. And in that moment when you are deciding between the knife and the gun, or the more complicated possibilities of poison, the phone rings. It is he. Nay, it is He. He has read it. Moreover, He likes it.

Very slowly, the rage drains from your body, and this man, whose slow and infinitely painful demise you were planning with such relish only a moment ago, now becomes the object of your lifelong esteem and adoration. Such is the relationship of a writer and his agent.

What of the agent and his client? In a writer's view, it follows that a good agent must, at all times, be a willing target for his client's extremes of emotions. A good agent has to be a volunteer *killee*, and almost in the next moment an equally willing shrine. He must offer his throat to his client's knife with the same generosity as he tenders his feet for his adoration. In brief, he must be as paranoid as you are. A good agent will go out into the market-place and be aggressive where you would be timid, demanding where you would be grateful, arrogant where you would simply apologize. In other words he will be you, your alter ego. He will crystallize all those images of you that, in a writer's glass, are most darkly seen. In short, a good agent is a writer's whore, and if he can be all those things, he can also be your friend.

I was lucky enough some months ago to find such an agent. His name is Mark Lucas, and he works at Fraser & Dunlop. He's very young and new to agenting. He was once in publishing, so he is well acquainted with the market-place. He reads for his pleasure and is no writer *manqué*. He also likes to deal, which is in itself an advantage for it means he does not confine himself to writers whose work he admires. He will take on work that represents a challenge to sell. He is not hooked on the easy 10 per cent.

If you're starting out as a writer, take some time in choosing your agent. The agents may play a hard-to-get game, but never forget that there are many, many more literary agents in the world than there are good writers.

You have the right of choice, far more than the go-betweens. Never forget that, or else you will end up being grateful. There is nothing more banal than gratitude, and for a writer it leads to penury. So choose an agent who is as hungry as you are. Avoid the big conglomerates, those with easy blockbusters on their books who have little time and less inclination to push a novel that will not help their profits. Choose an agent with a small and interesting stable. And stay with him. For in time a good agent will learn to know your style and your thinking patterns and his editorial advice will be well worth heeding.

Some writers eschew agents altogether, and wheel and deal on their own. For myself, I feel it is enough to write a book without having the hassle of having to sell it too. I am happy enough to pay 10 per cent to someone who cares enough to sell me. In any case, for me an agent is a safety-valve. If I had no agent, I would wake up one morning, and who knows whom I would want to kill?

One of the livelier, richer, more successful literary agents in London is the American Ed Victor. I asked him how he'd reached his present eminence.

I went to Dartmouth College in the USA and then came to England to do an M.Litt. at Cambridge. I then went to work for an obscure branch of the Beaverbrook empire called Oldbourne Press which was producing an encyclopaedia of art. I began to churn out literary essays on Renaissance painting about which I knew nothing, getting all my information from other books. Bored, I decided that I wanted to get into book publishing. So I wrote letters. I got hold of a copy of the *Writers' and Artists' Yearbook* and wrote to all the members of the Publishers Association saying what a great guy I was, that I had degrees, was sensible and accomplished, that I'd read English so was sensitive and smart. I got a lot of answers saying no but one from Tim O'Keefe at MacGibbon & Kee saying, 'I don't have a job but do come and see me.' He took me to a pub in Grape Street and we talked and talked and talked.

Suddenly he said, 'George Weidenfeld.' I said, 'Who?' 'Don't you know who he is?' and I said, 'Never heard of him.' Tim had decided I would be perfect for him: 'He will adopt you like a long-lost son. Get on to him right away and go there.'

I wrote to the managing director and next day Nicolas Thompson rang up to say, 'We do actually have a job editing coffee-table art books so come in for an interview.' At the interview, Nicolas was far more nervous than I. He enquired what sort of salary I was looking for. Cutting my throat I growled, 'Well, I'm twenty-four years old, I have a wife who is pregnant and about to give birth in February, I have a B.A. and an M.Litt., I'm experienced: I have got to have a thousand pounds a year.' There was a long silence. He gulped, 'I think we can manage that but a lot of the applicants require far less. Are you saying, you wouldn't come for less?' 'I wouldn't come for less,' I replied firmly and got the job. A thousand pounds a year seemed like a fortune in 1963; it was heady stuff.

I worked happily for a year, filling the gap left by Nigel Nicolson. I learnt how books were put together, which everybody should learn who wants to go into publishing, even attending a polytechnic to understand the details about production, which has always stood me in good stead.

Then one day in 1965, I suddenly looked around the company and saw that all the action was with the exciting new novelists they were publishing, with Mary McCarthy, Saul Bellow, Nabokov, Margaret Drabble and Dan Jacobson, who was pretty hot then, whilst all I was doing was these coffee-table books. I bumped into George Weidenfeld shortly after in the men's room and said that I would like to talk to him about moving over to the general books to which he replied 'Fine.' I was asked to breakfast at that amazing baroque house he had in Eaton Square. He only kept me waiting for an hour and a half. I had a boiled egg then said that I wanted to participate in the company's exciting ventures. He thought I was making a mistake; to him the future lay in co-editions but he agreed that I could move over and work for a while under Barley Alison.

George's company was then like a court, he was the Tsar around whom his courtiers revolved. People would leap out of the dark, stab others, whereupon new people would move forward closer to the Tsar. I moved up very quickly. Soon I was the blue-eyed boy, jetting off to New York to buy books. I was thrown in the deep end which was very good.

After three and a half years at Weidenfeld, I joined Jonathan Cape for three years and then, thirty years old, fat and unhappy, I left publishing to start a newspaper with Richard Neville who had created *OZ*. *INK* was not a success so I went to work for Bob Gottlieb at Knopf in New York for a while. As I had done all my publishing in England, working in America was like looking at everything through a slightly distorted mirror, which disturbed and upset me. In England publishing houses are much smaller and if you are a big-time editor, which I think I was at Cape, you have access to all of the essential publishing processes. You are right there deciding what sort of jacket a book will have, how many will be printed, how the reps will handle it, for you are the publisher. Whereas in America, if you are an editor, you are just that and no more. There was a long corridor at Knopf with many doors, behind each sat an editor; all we were expected to do was to bring in manuscripts, then hand them over to Bob or Tony or Nina to print, publicize and publish.

A major literary agent when I had been working at Weidenfeld's and at Cape's had been George Greenfield of John Farquharson, so on my return to England I went to him for advice. He asked me if I had ever thought of being an agent to which I said yes. 'Would you like to think of becoming one now?' 'No.' Whereupon Greenfield enquired 'Why not?' 'Because,' I replied, 'I don't think agents do what I want to do which is actually to make books.' He suggested that I go away and think about it, which I did and in 1974 I started work with him.

Then I decided to set up on my own so I started this company with a £15,000 overdraft and a decision to go all out to make money. Although I have an academic background, I love reading literary novels and I decided to go ahead and make money for my authors.

Agents can make money whereas publishers find this difficult, for they are usually paid a salary on a PAYE basis. I wanted to prove to myself that I could make money. Once I had proved that to my satisfaction it no longer interested me. Now I look for the action, which is in commercial books as they have huge phenomenal rights that you can sell. There are people who think up ideas which are marketable, authors who write well and whose second serial rights I can be selling years later. Irving Wallace for instance earned over two million dollars . . .

I have a list of authors all of whose work I handle. As well as Irving Wallace, I have Erich Segal and Roman Polanski, then I have up-and-coming people on my list who I am trying to make big. The middle ground has disappeared over the last year; when I compared last year's primary English contracts with the year before, the number had dropped from eighty to about forty, but I've made much more money.

To be a good agent you have to be good at making marriages, at introducing. You must find a publisher for whom the author you are offering will be *the* book for this year. The trick is finding the gaps, then asking the publisher for 'the highest sensible sum'; enough to make him worry but not panic; make him give the book all he's got. For instance, I was sent a first novel by a 47-year-old New Zealander, G. J. Scrimgeour, called *Woman of her Times*. I read two pages before lunch and decided immediately it was a winner. I rang Phyllis Grann at Putnams in America as she had mentioned that she had a gap in her spring list for a novel. She accepted it. I then sent the manuscript round to Philippa Harrison at Michael Joseph Ltd, as an arrival present – very important for new editors – and she paid £12,500 for it. Eventually *Woman of her Times* was the main selection of the Literary Guild: Pocket Books paid $225,000 for the American paperback rights and Pan £48,000 for paperback rights over here. I sold the French rights for F60,000 and the Spanish for $16,000.

An agent's job is to make things happen: to spin a book into orbit: to cut the filly out of the herd. Why, I once sold the Latvian rights of a book to a group of Latvians in New York but *excluding* Latvia itself. Give authors first-class treatment and publishers treat you in a first-class way.

Ed Victor underwent an initial apprenticeship in publishing before setting up on his own as a literary agent; Deborah Rogers jumped straight into agency work.

I was looking for somewhere to live in New York when I bumped into Lynn Nesbit, who later became my lucky break. After eighteen months in America I bummed around the world for a year. Back in England, desperate for a job, I wrote to half a dozen agents, ending up with Peter Janson Smith, Curtis Brown's foreign rights supremo from whom I learnt an incredible amount: his alertness to overseas markets made me very aware of all their ramifications.

Eventually I set up as a literary agent on my own. I got off to a good start because Lynn Nesbit asked me to represent her in England and by now she had become the hottest agent in New York. I had another piece of luck when I ran into Ann Warnford-Davis (now married to Tom Rosenthal lately of Secker & Warburg) in the street one day. She'd been the grand lady of foreign rights at Collins but had left to have a child. Two days later I telephoned her. She leapt at the chance of working for me from home and has been absolutely wonderful at arranging all our foreign rights ever since; without her I'd be lost.

In many ways it is easier for women to succeed as literary agents than as publishers; being a fairly new profession, there is less hierarchy to break through than in publishing. Publishers can be very stuffy. There was one who enraged me when I worked for Peter. He would ask me for help over small details, but if he wished to negotiate, even if it was a book of mine, he would always expect to speak to Peter. I still haven't forgotten that 'take me to your master' attitude of his . . . I don't do much with that publisher now.

> It's a fascinating life covering a whole range of people. There'll always be someone working on a book which is taking four or five years, someone who is producing two or three books a year, others who have got stuck or who need ideas. I always try to keep track of the lonely plodder for I realize how isolated he must feel. Sometimes writers are pushed for money and need helping out. Five or six publishers, who it would be unfair to name, are slow payers and some poor writers cannot afford to wait. If I feel strongly about a work and see that it is suffering, I may support the author for a while without a contract, but never for great sums of money.

Literary agents see authors through stony patches, disentangle their finances, help them with the Inland Revenue, find outlets for their work, hold their hands when the going gets rough and discourage them from writing books about Latin America ('there are only two things to know about publishing: books about Nelson always sell, books about Latin America never do' – the late Jonathan Cape). There are some prolific writers who scribble not only books, but short stories, film scripts, television plays and general journalistic articles; a good agency will find homes for all these offerings, tie up the contracts, check the royalty statements, see that their authors are entered for suitable prizes and given due deference by their publishers.

But how should a writer go about choosing a literary agent? I returned to Toby Eady to ask his opinion.

> You want professional advice so think clearly about what you are looking for in your literary agent. Would you prefer a young agent in a big firm or an independent individual? Find out if he has access to *all* the different markets of journalism, television, radio, publishers and film and check which are his specialist areas. Ask him how many clients he has; over forty successful writers would be rather much for one agent to handle competently. Now that publishers have cut back their editorial staff, you may need initial help in constructing your book so that it is in its best shape, can

the agent you are thinking of using edit? Don't forget that less than 1 per cent of books published do not need editing, although you may blench at the thought.

Make sure your prospective agent can read a balance sheet, a royalty statement and a contract and is able to ask a publisher how much of his turnover is out in unearned advances. Choose someone who is respected for his firmness and integrity, who sells to a variety of publishers and understands the international market. Find one who knows New York and visits there at least once a year, someone who can sell your work abroad and collect the money due to you from those markets and can deal with foreign tax forms. Find out what percentage he will charge you. Ten per cent is still standard but some agents are now charging 15 per cent for United Kingdom and Commonwealth sales and between 10 per cent and 15 per cent for sales to America and 20 per cent for foreign-language deals. Check whether his price includes a foreign agent's commission and whether or not he will charge you for copies of your book, postage and phone calls made on your behalf.

Choose someone who will answer the telephone with pleasure when you call, who will ring you once a month to find out how you are, what you are doing. Above all find someone who loves your work, likes you and knows how to sell your work, not just in England but internationally. But do remember that the best deal may not be the most money up front. If you think that, you will be changing agents and publishers continually.

## *Literary agents*

Here is my own brief list of literary agents who might be willing to help aspiring writers if approached with caution by letter first. A much fuller and more comprehensive one can be found in the *Writers' and Artists' Yearbook* published by A. & C. Black at £4.50 and fully revised in 1984. Agents are also listed in Cassell's *Directory of Publishing*. I trust no one will be offended by my eclectic selection, which is merely a personal choice.

GILLON AITKEN LTD
17 South Eaton Place, London SW1
The gentleman's agent, with a chic list including V. S. Naipaul and Paul Theroux, and this author. Recently, with Brian Stone, acquired Hughes Massie, whose bread, butter and caviare is the Agatha Christie Estate.

JACINTHA ALEXANDER
47 Emperor's Gate, London SW7
Trained at Curtis Brown and A. M. Heath, a friendly, independent agent operating out of her flat; clients include Brian Masters, Sian James and Christopher Warwick.

RUPERT CREW LTD
King's Mews, London WC1
Doreen Montgomery and Shirley Russell. These two ladies, homely in the English sense and always breaking their diets, operate one of the smartest literary agencies in London. They will not say how much Barbara Cartland earns but her last cheque from France was for six figures. Originally Mr Crew launched Godfrey Winn and they go in for romance and oddities like Robert Harbin, the Origami fellow. A good home for romantic fictionereens like Dinah Lampitt.

CURTIS BROWN
162–8 Regent Street, London W1
Perhaps the oldest and the biggest. After a hiccup in City ownership it is now its own master and has absorbed James Oliver Brown in New York and merged with John Farquharson in London, whose founder in 1919 was a former employee. George Greenfield specializes in travel and adventure; they have an academic side originated by Andrew Best and a glittering list of clients.

TOBY EADY
55 Great Ormond Street, London WC1
Rugged individualist on his own. Has lived eight years in New

York so knows the American scene at first hand. David Taylor (q.v.) is one of his newest recruits.

A. M. HEATH & CO. LTD
40 William IV Street, London WC2
Dependable, long-lasting agency now run by Mark Hamilton and Michael Thomas. Linked with Brandt & Brandt in America.

A. D. PETERS & CO. LTD
10 Buckingham Street, London WC2
Headed by the political and rebarbative Michael Sissons and his partner Pat Kavanagh. A list of stars which includes the intelligence expert Nigel West and the novelist Isabel Colegate. Younger authors are carefully tended by Caroline Dawnay.

DEBORAH ROGERS LTD
49 Blenheim Crescent, London W11
The most successful agent of the decade. Strong European links, ditto high lit., e.g. Angela Carter, Bruce Chatwin, Ian McEwan and Salman Rushdie.

SCOTT FERRIS ASSOCIATES
15 Gledhow Gardens, London SW5
Gloria Ferris was for years Doubleday's 'man in London'. Big-hearted – good for new authors. Rivers Scott was formerly literary editor of the *Sunday Telegraph* and *Now!*, and publisher at Hodder & Stoughton.

ABNER STEIN
10 Roland Gardens, London SW7
Another American moving into the big-time.

ED VICTOR LTD
162 Wardour Street, London W1
Stylish, big-time American wheeler-dealer. The other most successful agent of the decade.

A. P. WATT LTD
26 Bedford Row, London WC1
Started in 1875. Claim to be the oldest literary agency. Run by author-agent Hilary Rubinstein. They still make money

out of writers like Rider Haggard, Kipling, Baroness Orczy, Rafael Sabatini and Somerset Maugham and today handle Nadine Gordimer and Frederic Raphael.

# III *Publishers*

The true publisher is an eternal enthusiast, possessed of exceptional curiosity. He longs to know what lies inside each and every new manuscript that drops on to his desk; he opens each with excitement, hoping it will be a masterpiece. Knowledge, time and experience never dim his optimism. He chooses to publish those books he likes or imagines will be successful. His choice is inevitably subjective.

Some publishers are egomaniacs, always talking about 'my' authors, 'my' books, but the more honest members of the trade admit they are but middlemen printing, producing, publicizing and promoting the creative work of others. 'The book belongs to the person who wrote it. It is always the author's book, all we are doing is marketing it for him,' says Sonny Mehta of Pan. On the whole publishers are not, in a commercial sense, aggressive towards each other.

When Harold Pinter came to see me, wearing a feather in his hat, which he didn't take off, to ask me to publish *The Caretaker*, I explained that I didn't do plays but suggested that he go to Methuen instead. They have since sold thousands of copies. In turn I received my best English textbook, *English Through Experience*, which has taught two-thirds of Britain, from Heinemann. Horses for courses.

Publishing is one of the most varied commercial enterprises: the potential scope for any single firm is huge. Such diversification enables those involved to express their individuality and taste, to play the impresario over a wide area. To become a publisher is to enter a high-risk field of endeavour, to court danger and to gain wide publicity; there are more column inches in the press devoted to those in publishing than to those who make socks or soft drinks. If your taste happens to coincide with others who will pay to read it, you may even make money. But this is a gamble and it is the irrationality, the fickleness of the book-buying public which makes publishing so stimulating.

Anyone can start up a firm on his own, in his kitchen. All he has to do is either to write a book himself or find a friend who has done so, get it printed locally and hawk it around the bookshops. At the other end of the scale are the big battalions whose turnovers are measured in millions. For instance, Octopus made a profit of £4.8 million in 1982 and Collins's published figure was only slightly less. Penguin (part of the S. Pearson group) were 42 per cent up at £5.64 million. Associated Book Publishers, which include Methuen, E. & F. N. Spon, Chapman & Hall and Eyre & Spottiswoode, were greatly helped by their *Dictionary of Organic Compounds* in America and by excellent Canadian sales so they were able to announce a 38 per cent rise in profits from £4m to £5.6 million. All S. Pearson's know-how did not stop Longmans having a poor year, plagued by reduced trading in Nigeria, write-offs and bad debts; Routledge & Kegan Paul also did badly. In some firms, one book may make all the difference; it looks as if about 4 per cent of Hodder & Stoughton's turnover is provided by Jeffrey Archer, since they publish both his hardback and paperback versions. Faber's cash flow has been helped by what they have received from the musical *Cats*, which is based on a work by their former director, T. S. Eliot; it has become their North Sea oil. Backlists can also keep firms going in bad times, though millions of volumes stacked in serried ranks in warehouses can just tie up capital, leaving none for new authors.

To try to give some idea of the variety of this glamorous, irrational, risky but exhilarating trade, I have talked to some publishers and give next jottings made from conversations. They include old, famous firms and new ones, large ones and small. I'll begin with John Brown, whose father Sir John (Bruno) Brown secured for the Oxford University Press the biggest bestseller in the world, *The Advanced English Learner's Dictionary*, originally published in Tokyo in 1942. (Many might name The Bible as *the* bestseller, but the holy Book is put out in a variety of editions.)

John Brown is an amiable, garrulous and cheeky chappie who represents the authentic voice of the younger generation in publishing on both sides of the Atlantic, innovative, iconoclastic, mobile and tieless, his offices were a far cry from his father's marble halls. Sir John Brown had been publisher to the oldest, grandest imprint in the world, that of the Oxford University Press, whose London office was once the palace of the Bishop of Ely. The son worked up a fire escape in a Soho mews, his offices had the quality of an illegal book-making – rather than a book-publishing – establishment when I visited him. He explained how he came to be there.

> I went to the London College of Printing at the age of eighteen, where you don't have to be clever at all: it was a pushover. I was paid for by the government and got an extremely good business studies education; I had a short stint in America then alternated six months in London with six months in Oxford for three years.
>
> In Oxford I was with the University Press's printing division where I learnt a great deal about office politics. I also learnt basic printing techniques, all of which could have been acquired in five days. As it was, I worked three days on each machine; as most of the machines were identical, I spent an enormous amount of time sitting around doing absolutely nothing which taught me to get on with people who were not of the same background, same age or same type as me when I was theoretically the boss's son.
>
> I had gone into printing with the naive idea that it was artistic but soon found out it was just manufacturing. Neither art nor skill were involved, I was just a machine minder. However, I didn't want to reject three years' invest-

ment so when I'd finished my apprenticeship I decided to look for a job where I could use my experience.

I went into the production side of Hutchinson's for ten months. It was extremely boring, extremely tiresome, Radlett is a loathable place. However, I did learn how much everything cost and how much profit was made. I was given a book, told how many pages it was to have and then told to get it printed. All I had to do was to make sure that the printing was good and that it was finished on time. I saw the core of publishing, how it does or doesn't make money. Although publishing is not about making money, you have to make money to *stay* in publishing.

Then I joined Jonathan Cape to chase the sales force and generally assist their Publicity and Art Director Tony Colwell. He certainly taught me that advertising was rarely worth it.

After a couple of years I went to see the boss, who was a pretty groovy guy. [Graham Greene, nephew of the eponymous writer, quondam President of the Publishers Association, a stately rather than a groovy figure to my mind.] He said he thought there were jobs going at Faber's. I wasn't that keen to go into an old-fashioned firm: in fact I knew I'd hate it but I thought maybe I ought to go. Then I heard through someone that there was a job going at Eel Pie Publishing owned by Pete Townshend the pop star. I like a bit of glamour so it got me very excited. I found the details in the *Bookseller* and went after the job.

I joined the company as trainee sales manager. There were about ten of us altogether. After two days I became *the* sales manager because it was soon apparent that I had more publishing experience than the rest of the company put together. Editorially the company was being run by Matthew Price, a brilliant children's book editor, and he'd just introduced a couple of rock books, but it was all in complete shit because no one had any experience.

We did these couple of rock books which went well but in March 1981 the money ran out. There were about five Eel Pie companies, including a bookshop, a video company and some studios and I thought all were done for, which was a shame because the books we'd been doing had been good quality. They weren't sold well, they weren't marketed well, they weren't distributed well, they weren't publicized well and a great deal of money was wasted, but the books were good. We had a reputation for being eccentric but interesting; much money had been pissed down the drain but it would have been a great shame if we'd gone under. However, we survived in truncated form. We went from ten people to four: Matthew Price, myself, an editor and a secretary, and began to publish about sixteen books a year.

We changed from doing mainly children's books and a few rock books to mainly rock and a few children's, then we cut out all the dodgy books like *How to Choose a Guru*. When Matthew Price left, we upped our rock book programme, which was the side I enjoyed most. It was profitable and an area of the market which no one else was exploiting.

We use plenty of freelance people which works very well because however rich we become we hope never to fall into that big-company pit of flinging shit against the wall to see what sticks, like Hutchinson, where overheads are huge and they employ so many people that they just have to publish three hundred books a year to keep everyone occupied. At the moment four of us are producing sixteen books a year, 80 per cent on rock, 10 per cent of which we sell through record shops, otherwise we sell through absolutely straight outlets, although that strange shop Forbidden Planet does well with our books, amongst its science fiction mags and posters.

Unlike other publishers who may do the odd rock book on the side, we are first and foremost rock book publishers; this makes us ten steps ahead. People come to us in the first place because we know what we are talking about. Our editor and general atmosphere is much more sympathetic to someone who has written a rock book – let us say a rock journalist. Big publishers in drab offices may have bigger sales forces, larger publicity and foreign rights departments but they make the rock author feel alienated.

What's more, we earn our authors more money. We sold our first rock book for $100,000 advance and our second as a package for $200,000.

In 1984 I hope we'll expand to produce twenty-five books and then level off so that by 1985 we could survive on five really good books. In a company of our size you either expand or decrease your operation to a specific book; you build up a gig.

We get reviews in *Melody Maker*, *Honey*, *Cosmo* and *NME*, and in the rock press itself more space is given to Eel Pie books than any other publisher, but the heavies never touch our sort. The *Sunday Times* will devote half a page to Stockhausen or some obscure play which can interest few readers yet will only give half a paragraph once a fortnight to some well-known rock group whose music is immensely popular.

We are catering to youth culture. The everyday English publishing scene is quite good at what it does but it never expands: in Germany there are ten or fifteen publishers like Eel Pie, two or three in America and a few in France. Soon I hope we will be making films and videos.

All this is, alas, perhaps typically, in the past tense now, for Pete Townshend sold stock in Eel Pie a few weeks after this interview and is now reputed to be introducing Faber & Faber to rock and pop. John Brown moved to Virgin Books.

But John Brown's own story is not over; this is, I am sure, only the first chapter in what will undoubtedly be an illustrious career. His tale does, however, pertinently illuminate certain interesting facets of the publishing scene: its seemingly glamorous image to the young; the excitement and challenge of finding authors among your own generation who are also starting out in life and whom you feel you can help; the ebullience of small firms, their daring and ingenuity; the wide variety of choice within the industry and the way people move from one firm to another up a career ladder.

For contrast I went to see John Brown's father's old firm, where Robin Denniston is now the Academic and General

Publisher to the Oxford University Press. Secretary to the Delegates and Chief Executive is George Richardson.

Commenting on the professionalism and commercialism of the last decade, Robin Denniston said, 'Publishers have "learned the money" for themselves and lost something in the process.' The change in the conduct of England's oldest publishing house during the last decade mirrors with surprising accuracy the changes in the trade generally. Surprising, because one might not expect a venerable institution to behave with such lack of ruth until it is noted that charities, churches and gentlemen's clubs, not to speak of synagogues, often behave more heartlessly towards their employees than big business. Not that there is anything heartless about Mr Denniston, an admirable workhorse of a publisher who spent ten years with Collins, thirteen with Hodders as Managing Director, two with Weidenfeld and a miserable three as supremo of the imprints of the Thomson Organization: Michael Joseph, Hamish Hamilton, Rainbird, Nelson and Sphere. His has been the classic professional publisher's career with the dashing additive that, since his father founded and ran the secret code-breaking outfit at Bletchley during the war (for which he received no recognition whatsoever), he has enjoyed, in the way that other publishers have suffered, his encounters with the Ministry of Defence and the notorious D-notice committee. It was he who published F. W. Winterbotham's *Ultra Secret* in 1974, thus breaking the long, long silence on the Enigma code-breakers.

At Hodders, he lured Le Carré from Heinemann by paying a great deal for one of his least successful books, *Naive and Sentimental Lover*, published Anthony Sampson, his friend from schooldays, and Francis Chichester. Now he laments the passing of the sixties, when he could have fun, afford a few failures and make money if he published enough with flair, with luck. Perhaps he forgets that in those days he had a message pinned to his desk for his personal contemplation, which read 'I am not Tom Maschler, I am not Tony Godwin', naming two whizzers of that swinging era.

Robin Denniston supervised the amalgamation of OUP's London division, devoted to books which were supposed to make money, with the Clarendon Press in Walton Street, Oxford, which was less commercial, supposed as it was by its owners, the Delegates of the University, to illumine the darker reaches of academe. There was an obvious clash between these two enterprises which Denniston harmonized. He appreciated that, with the present cost of warehousing and interest rates, the old publishing doctrine, which says that a house depends on a strong backlist, no longer holds. Indeed, current analysis shows that a publisher's most profitable books are those he is going to publish tomorrow and not the ones of yesterday, lingering in some musty barn selling a steady twenty-two copies a month – fifteen years' supply.

He has been with OUP since 1979, in which year, for the first time in its history, the Press made a loss. 1980 was also a poor year, but sales and profits improved in 1981 and in 1982. In the year ending March 1983, profits were £5.2 million on a turnover of £67.6 million, a rise of 18 per cent. All along the corridors of this vast publishing emporium are graphs showing the sales figures of each section, all are zooming straight for the stars.

The begowned delegates of OUP, mainly heads of colleges, meet in conclave twice a month to decide which academic manuscripts will ultimately carry that intellectual accolade, a Clarendon imprint. These are often erudite monographs, fifty-year histories on defined topics such as *The Development of Creole Society in Jamaica 1770–1820* in paperback at £8.95 for example, which will be bought mainly by libraries. The Press has become adept at bringing these out at very low prices *and* making ends meet on a printing of only 850 copies. This is made possible by negotiating with the author for a deferred royalty payment and by having the book set by local women in their own homes. These Oxfordshire worthies, Ann Joshua is one, have revolutionized the face of academic publishing because they set through IBM typewriters on their kitchen table for £5.50 a page, even complex mathematical formulae. They correct the proofs and then the book itself can be printed and bound either abroad, locally or in OUP's own printing works. A unit cost of £3 for 850 copies is thus possible. Forty per cent of this print run might be sold in the

United States before publication at 62 per cent discount perhaps 100 copies will be sold in the British Isles, 80 in Europe, 30 in Japan, 10 in Australia and 5 in Canada with a hundred or so going to the Middle and Far East if it is of medical interest. The Oxford University Press have thus already moved into the future. Newer methods of computer setting will not further lower the price of these books for some years: the system may get quicker but will probably not save much money for another decade or so.

The Reverend Robin Denniston, for he is an Anglican priest and also a Student of Christ Church, took me on a guided tour of the vast building, built round a quadrangle like some huge college. Long, dark corridors have cell-like rooms opening off on either side in which sit the specialists devoted to music and to lexicography, to finance and overseas sales, to economics and aids to English teaching. On and on we went up stairs, down tunnels marked 'No Ball Games allowed here', past vast printing machines, computers, binders and piles of examination questions for West African schoolchildren. Lost in a maze of back alleys, we finally climbed a fire-escape and re-entered the block through someone's window, tumbling over the desk and dropping to the floor with a thud, much to the occupier's astonishment.

But this huge, multi-faceted conglomerate is no slouch. Its prices are competitive; it even prints for other publishers. It offers authors handsome advances up to six figures for newly commissioned works, its growing medical and science departments produce over 230 books a year, it runs a music hire library and has a hymn copyright department; indeed it is one of the four top music publishers in this country, churning out all Vaughan Williams's and William Walton's works. It has an American section, one of whose top dollar-producers is Tygiel's *Baseball's Great Experiment*, and a lexicographic set-up deep in computers for updating dictionaries, with video and tape machines to check up on the latest TV and radio chat programmes: the new word baffling the boffins at the moment is 'wally' – when did it first appear and where?

But it is in the realm of English language teaching books that OUP is supreme. One title alone, *The Advanced English*

*Learner's Dictionary* (q.v.), has sold over 600,000 copies each year, every year, for the last ten years. During that time Greece and Spain have not been backward in buying but Germany has had over a million and Nigeria has swallowed over two and a half million copies.

Most publishers have been burned selling to Nigeria (Evans went wrong after the *coup*), but OUP is still carrying on. Their sales there are a fifth of what they were three years ago, and much less than in the heady oil boom years of the early seventies, but they live in hopes of a rosier future. It may be hard to get bills paid but OUP are not about to throw away all those years of effort to competitors.

Robin Denniston sees it as his prime duty to survive: 'the University would not save us if they could, they have better things to do with their money.' This is not at all the sort of language his predecessor Sir John Brown would have used to describe the function of the Press fifteen years ago. Their mission, formerly to follow the University's motto 'The Lord is my Light' and to propagate knowledge throughout the world, has become a simpler need to survive. With profits over five million they could be said to be just about managing.

The withdrawal of the Press to Oxford has resulted in environmental as well as economic benefits. 'It's very agreeable', says Robin, 'to walk across the fields to work,' and this view is shared by two of his most brilliant editors, Ron Heapy, head of children's books, and Richard Charkin, head of reference, who would not for any money come back to London.

Change, movement, new heads; publishing firms, like any other commercial enterprise, flourish, fade or fall according to the luck and skill of those at the helm. Successful firms riding high anxiously seek bright young things to train to be Grand Panjandrums of the future. If they cannot find someone suitable, they may have to sell their list to another firm. Roger Pocklington Senhouse, squire of Maryport, Cumbria, joined Fredric Warburg in 1936 to buy Martin Secker's list, which included Norman Douglas, Thomas Mann and Kafka; this formed the nucleus of the new firm to which Senhouse, with his literary talent, added greater lustre: Warburg was the publicist. Cautiously entering his Dickensian room in John Street (having been bombed out of the Adelphi), Roger would wend his way through Lytton Strachey's library piled in stacks up to the Henry Moores on the walls, to his round rent table where he would fastidiously dip his pen into purple ink in order to correct Angus Wilson's English, to translate Colette, to write to Eithne or Ernst Kaiser (translators of Robert Musil), or to correspond with André Gide. Pseudonymously he put Jean Genet's *Querelle de Brest* into such exquisitely accurate 1930s queer slang that it was not understood by the American publishers, who refused to use it. Senhouse epitomized the old-fashioned publisher: he cared about authors, especially poets; he had high intellectual and academic standards, he sought the best. It was immaterial to him whether or not the books made money: someone would always put capital into the firm to publish recognizable excellence. He was right, someone always did. First William Heinemann Ltd, then Thomas Tilling, from their road haulage nationalization money, and now BTR.

As old age set in, Roger Senhouse retired to Brighton, only to be plagued by Michael Holroyd, who needed Roger's imprimatur before he could publish his biography of Lytton Strachey. Meanwhile, Fredric Warburg looked round for a successor. He had no desire to sell his authors off to some new arrival, preferring to train a young man up in his own image. First he chose Norman St John Stevas because of his high degrees from Cambridge and from Oxford, his prizes and his scholarship, his legal brilliance and his unique knowledge of *Obscenity and the Law*, but after a year at Secker & Warburg, the lure of politics proved too strong. A succession of young men followed, including Eric Newby, Graham C. Greene, Maurice Temple Smith and Tom Rosenthal but none really replaced Fred. Today Peter Grose, an Australian, holds the fort, which has a keep for Barley Alison's private imprint, where Piers Paul Read and Saul Bellow are the crown jewels.

With this example before them, Chatto & Windus hunted hard for a successor for Norah Smallwood. Chatto & Windus was a hundred years old in 1955. The real founder of the firm was a Cornish whirlwind called John Camden Hotten who set up in Piccadilly as a bookseller/publisher, just where the Ritz is now. Hotten really knew what publishing was about. In 1864 his list included a fine edition of *The Book of Common Prayer*, a *Guide to Stamp Collecting*, a cookbook by the confectioner of Gunters and a *History of Flogging*. He had also been to America, spotted and published Mark Twain and, in retaliation for the Americans' piracy of Charles Dickens, paid, originally, no royalties. Mr Hotten's widow (he died young at 43) sold the business to a Mr Andrew Chatto who brought in Mr W. E. Windus, a literary gentleman of small interest.

However, the firm became the famous partnership in publishing with probably the most distinguished literary list in London at the time, with authors like Alexander Herzen, Proust, Stevenson and Strachey. More recently V. S. Pritchett and D. J. Enright joined their company, also Iris Murdoch and Dirk Bogarde (now with Allen Lane), Norah Smallwood's discoveries. She was succeeded by that equally powerful publisher Carmen Callil.

Carmen hit London from Australia in 1960. She was 'a dumpy little thing with a colonial accent and an inferiority complex', her words. Bored by working for Marks & Spencer, she moved into publishing and worked briefly in menial positions at Hutchinsons and Batsfords. She then graduated to doing publicity for Granada Publishing, André Deutsch and briefly for Anthony Blond, before starting her own book publicity company. Working on the ill-fated underground newspaper *INK*, founded by Ed Victor *et al.*, she met her first feminists and saw the light. With £1,500, friendly advice from printer and publisher Bob Gavron and from his friend and hers, Paul Hamlyn, the megalopublisher of immemorabilia, she started Virago Press (telegraphic address Caterwaul). It was an overtly feminist operation both in product and personnel. Harriet Spicer was with her from the start. They were joined first by Ursula Owen and later Kate Griffin, who agreed to be the best sales person in London. The author, when interviewing this tricky subject, was foolish enough to demur that surely somewhere was a man, the art director perhaps? 'I choose the covers and I am not a man,' asserted Callil.

Apart from initiating original, high quality feminist literature, of which Pat Barker's *Union Street* is a good example, as it sold 10,000 copies in paperback at £2.95 and could also be obtained bound for public libraries at £7.50, Virago has been so successful in reissuing classics in lively format that by 1981 it turned over £600,000. Now all that expertise and ability has been unleashed upon Chatto's.

While I was talking to her, an interior decorator appeared with some swatches of material. Would Miss Callil like to choose new covers for her office chairs? She pretended to ask my opinion and changed her mind nine times – but very quickly.

Carmen Callil, a lady of some forty springs, looks as if she will last for many a summer. She is absolutely right for the decade and if she cannot steer the stately old vessel of Chatto & Windus through the shoals of recession, nobody can.

Another grand old ship which had a bad buffeting in the 1970s but which has triumphed in the 1980s under decisive modern leadership is William Collins Ltd, helmed by Ian Chapman.

In the war, Ian Chapman moved from the RAF to become a 'Bevin boy', from high in the sky to deep underground, where, as he puts it, 'being ambitious, I hewed the coalface'. His publishing career has the same unvaried verticality. From trainee sales manager in Collins in 1947 to Chairman at £50,000 a year, a modest salary considering he controls a turnover of £100 million, he might be said to be the most powerful man in the British book business.

If the publishing world is a stage Ian Chapman might at first be mistaken for a bit player. He is without the polyglot, highly social theatricality of George Weidenfeld or the Bauhaus Ritziness of Paul Hamlyn (whose flotation of Octopus in April 1983 netted him £17 million and made two of his employees cigar-smoking millionaires in one minute). Ian Chapman is a quiet non-smoker standing firmly on the quarterdeck of Collins, the flagship of British publishing. Unlike the fatally exposed Nelson, he has always avoided publicity and perhaps this attribute, together with his tact and agility, enabled him to acquire in April 1983, in total secrecy – publishing is a highly rumourous activity – all Sidney Bernstein's Granada imprints for £12 million gross but more like £8.5 million net. To his own Fontana and Flamingo he has now added Dragon, Mayflower, Paladin, Panther, nautical Adlard Coles and the educational lists of Chatto & Windus, Hart-Davis and MacGibbon and Kee.

At the same time the firm moved from St James's Place to Grafton Street in Mayfair where, symbolically, a staid eighteenth-century façade fronts a modern, seven-storey office block. Here Ian Chapman literally and metaphorically presides at the top whilst his wife works as an editor on the floor below.

The company has come a long way since 1842, when a former Collins put in his bookseller's window this little jingle which Ian Chapman discovered in the archives:

Holy Bible writ divine
Bound in leather 1/9.
Satan trembles
When he sees
Bibles sold as cheap as these.

Incidentally, Bibles, like tobacco and contraceptives, may not be advertised on television. The Act of Parliament which allowed only the Privileged Presses at Oxford University, Cambridge University and Messrs Eyre & Spottiswoode to publish the Authorized Version in England did not apply to Scotland; the Collins fortunes were built on the backs of the Holy Writ, diaries, stationery and printing, until the late Sir William, better known as 'Billy', came south and with the aid of his lady wife moved the family business into big-time general publishing. Now Collins publish every category from archaeology to westerns and put out more bestsellers than anyone in London. They have the biggest crime list, dominated of course by Agatha Christie, their first big author, who is an industry in her own right.

Ian Chapman is lying down peacefully with Rupert Murdoch, whose News International plc is the largest single shareholder of Collins, so the flagship is set fair on its course perhaps in the direction of the USA? But Ian Chapman is unlikely to change the tone of the firm, being more of a middlebrow traditionalist than a revolutionary, and certainly no carpetbagger. He claims to allow his editors complete freedom but he cannot help behaving like a man of power He respects the virtues of continued author–publisher relationship and deplores, though he does not prevent, his company's participation in auctions.

But it is not necessary to be a grand old house of long standing to have built up a huge list and to publish a large number of books. It is possible today to explode instantly upon the scene a star bursting into nova, like Anthony Cheetham, founder of Century, the newest imprint in Britain. 'The City,' said Anthony, 'loves publishing. Mind you, they don't always like the accounts and these are early days.' Indeed they were, for when he spoke to me his firm was only four days old, a lusty infant born on the fourth floor of a modern building in Soho Visiting him reminded me of my first day in publishing back in 1956, spent in the basement of a now-deceased house, with Allan Wingate (a mythical figure who never came in on Fridays to sign the cheques), cutting out an illustration captioned 'Spice and Vice in Soho' from every copy printed, as a lady had spotted herself in the picture, innocently buying an aubergine, and had successfully sued.

Anthony Cheetham, Eton and Balliol, whizz-kid of Abacus, bought *Small is Beautiful* when everyone in London said it had no paperback potential, then founded Futura where he published *The Thorn Birds*, a classic jumbo, then inevitably fell foul of Captain Maxwell when he bought the company, and so now runs his own new concern, Century. He has a fiction editor (Rosemary Cheetham), and her assistant, a non-fiction editor, Gail Rebuck, plus assistant, a publicist, a money man, a sales manager plus one assistant, and six representatives. He is pitching for a turnover of £6 million on a capital of £600,000 and hopes for a public flotation soon. For this he needs a hundred titles a year, most of which must be low-risk, low-print but three must be manufactured bestsellers – glossy set-books like *Cider with Rosie* and *Lark Rise to Candleford*.

'A jumbo', he told me, 'is like an elephant, it takes about three years to gestate. I brought Maeve Binchy with me from Macdonalds and we nourished her. The book is a hit. We will sell 20,000 copies and I've made a big paperback deal [published by Coronet in 1983, it sold 200,000 copies]. Publishing has changed in the last two years, paperbacks have diversified, gone upmarket with more illustrations and better jackets. Look at the success of Abacus, Picador, Paladin, Virago, Mermaid and Papermac. There is another tendency – de-internationalization' . . . (Anthony Cheetham is a very modern man, he often uses words like that and has a telephone system which can dial Australia by itself, which saves him a switch-girl) . . . 'de-internationalization means the growth of native wares. If you go to a bookshop in Sydney you won't see the same books you see in Foyles.'

Century's catalogue is elegant, professional, American in aspect – it leads with two jumbos and introduces a new high-tech list with computer software promise. There is also a series of fancy-looking paperbacks 'like Rolls-Royces printed on bloody fine paper at £4.95' and travel books by authors like Mark Twain, A. W. Kinglake and Freya Stark, which proves the publishing adage that a retread is often less of a commercial risk than an original. All you need is a dead author and a good art department. 'I don't have one,' says Anthony, 'there are hundreds of studios round here.' (Since this interview Century has moved to larger premises a few blocks over, where there *is* a switch-girl.)

'Each book must be treated as a separate publishing company,' he says, echoing John Brown of Eel Pie just down the road, who calls them 'a separate gig'. 'Nevertheless, if you are persistent you can make it with a series of middle-of-the-

road and lowbrow fiction. Robert Hale, who still publishe
two hundred novels a year, could be – should be – the mos
profitable publisher in London. Tom McCormack does th
same thing with St Martin's Press in New York with the sam
result.'

Maybe Mr Cheetham isn't walking down the same street
His firm is young, impatient and with it. The City gents wh
backed him will be pleased.

Throughout this book the name of George Weidenfeld crop
up again and again, for he is the grandest figure in Englis
publishing today. His influence throughout the entire trade i
immense because so many people in the business have so
journed for a while at his court and felt the burning flame o
his enthusiasm.

George Weidenfeld, who was once political advisor t
Chaim Weizmann and has published every major Israeli fron
Allon to Yadin, was born in Vienna in 1919. Once, when i
the elitist *Gymnasium* he was obliged to participate in a due
he maximized his incapacity by fighting left-handed. Thi
tactic threw his opponent. During his long, colourful and b
no means ended, career, he has won many battles. He i
a peer of the realm by courtesy of Harold Wilson, whon
he knew as an economics don at University College Oxfor
and early published, a pillar of the SDP, one of London'
more brilliant and frequent hosts and a dominator of his pub
lishing company, which with ICFC (24 per cent) he mainl
owns.

Weidenfeld & Nicolson Ltd occupy the top three floors o
a fairly high-rise, black-and-white glass building in Claphan
High Street. Here are housed all the different facets whicl
make up the whole group including their Arthur Barke
imprint, World University Library, trade and academic paper
backs, history and international economics series. It is thei
wont to hold acquisition meetings in their boardroom t
discuss projects for possible publication and on April 13th
1983 they allowed me to be present. Also there were Lor
Weidenfeld; John Curtis, Editor; Ray Compton, Managin
Director and financial supremo; Richard Hussey, Deput

Managing Director of production; John Gross, their ex-guru; Ros Lewis, Marketing and Publicity Director; Stephen du Sautoy of Arthur Barker Ltd; and Robert Baldock who runs Weidenfeld & Nicolson's academic list.

George Weidenfeld, who plainly enjoys the variety of his lists, and 'drives the beat' on these occasions (although he begged me to point out that many of the projects are initiated by his editors), opened the proceedings. The discussion centred around eighteen projects which had already been accepted for publication and more than fifty pending, all listed on tightly printed sheets with the copies of the project form distributed round the table. The form is neat and tells all you need to know: title, author, agent, number of words, delivery date, advance paid, royalty, share of subsidiary rights, unit price and published price. It does not show the contribution to overheads, nor the break-even point with and without overheads.

The fire is rapid. George opens up.

'This book by Bouer, a Czech, is a gamble at $5,000. I think I can get Hebrew and US publishing interest at the next fair on the back of the author's personality.

'Elizabeth Hardwick book. Problem here with Random House but Jason Epstein is on our side although we have to match Carmen Callil's offer of 2,500.' It is agreed that they should.

'A life of Kokoschka by a Thames & Hudson author.'

'A good man,' interjects John Gross. He is a former editor of *The Times Literary Supplement* so should know.

'Bob Thomas, author of our *Life of William Holden*, wants to do Fred Astaire. Good idea?' There is a mutter of agreement from everyone.

'Lord Chalfont's memoirs. OK?

'Abba Eban on Jewish civilization.' Short silence until George explains that PBS (television company) in America are basing thirteen 15-minute programmes on this subject with Eban as presenter. Then a lively discussion ensues at which it is resolved to commit the company to 7,500 if there is no UK television deal and 15,000 if there is. 'Dollars or copies?' asks Richard Hussey. 'Copies,' comes back the answer. George then remarks that the combination of the author's agent, Simon & Schuster, and their agent could be tricky.

'We are not interested, are we, in a book on the Princess of Wales?'

'We've already got one, George,' somebody moans.

'No, NO,' explains the chairman, 'this is different.' But at the name of the packager who has presented the project, the meeting shakes its head, and the idea is dropped.

Thus in a fast, friendly and ultimately fair way, each project is considered with equal emphasis irrespective of the clout, as it were, of the proposer. The meetings are obviously comradely, invigorating and, in a strange way, uplifting. They are also quite funny, although businesslike. One could say that human rather than financial interests engage the attention of the meeting more than, say, a group of people concerned with the manufacture of men's hose.

Announcing, 'I am going to have lunch with Martin Gilbert,' Lord Weidenfeld left the meeting and sped across the river in his immaculate white, chauffeur-driven Mercedes.

The exchanges I have just described were but a fraction of the comments given by the lively minds present at the meeting, all of whom advanced their opinion with temerity, irrespective of status, salary or position and I like to think such free and frank discussion is typical of what happens in the boardrooms of large, successful, post-war publishing firms. Typical too, however, of the volatility of the publishing scene and of Weidenfeld in particular, John Gross soon left to become literary editor of the *Spectator* for half an hour before joining the *New York Times* and Stephen du Sautoy has gone to run a bookshop.

Some depart and others arrive. A new presence on the English publishing scene, who has in many ways tried to emulate Lord Weidenfeld, is Naim Attallah of Quartet.

Sidney Bernstein, the lion from Romford, had strong views on every subject which were not always shared by William Miller, once London's cleverest and cuddliest paperback editor at Panther. The Granadan Labour lord of all he surveyed liked being on first-name terms with his senior editors. To

Villiam Miller he once said, 'Why don't you call me Sidney ike everybody else?' 'No, Lord Bernstein, I will not.' William ıpped sticks and left together with John Boothe and Ken 3anerji (Sales) and Brian Thompson to start a new imprint vhich they entitled Quartet. Backed by a group of well-heeled ınd well-bred young gentlemen who were 'something in the City', the list was designed to be vaguely up-market and to he left of Penguin. William Miller's taste, both eclectic and atholic (with the smallest of 'c's – he is a passionate republi-an and atheist with all the ferocity of an ex-choirboy), was een in the quality of Quartet authors: Lillian Hellman, Claud Cockburn, Colin Spencer and Sybille Bedford. However, lespite – or perhaps because of – this quality publishing, by 1976 Quartet was ailing, a condition barely mitigated by their erennial bestseller, Alex Comfort's *The Joy of Sex*.

Enter centre stage, brightly lit, with a smile and a rib-reaking hug, litigious, lovable Rolls-Royced Naim Attallah.

William Miller has a mind of his own, not a characteristic eople seem to search for in employees, so he was soon off o start a literary agency in Tokyo with a generous contract or a travel book within his Pakamac pocket. Naim got a ıew, if not totally shiny, toy to play with and the London ublishing scene, starved of eccentric proprietors since the lemise of Victor Gollancz, got someone to talk about.

Stories abound about Naim's past. Certainly it is true that ıe was spotted by Yussuf Bedas of Intra Bank and made a ortune out of foreign exchange. True, too, that he started up Asprey's in New York and became its joint managing director ılthough he owns no shares in the company. (One of his ıot-so-general titles, *A History of Asprey* by Bevis Hillier, eveals that John Betjeman's father spent his life in Asprey's vorkshop making ivory inlaid furniture for Maharajahs – rrelevant but surely interesting enough to merit an aside.)

Quartet works out of a pleasing chaos in Goodge Street. Through the corridors swirl elegant, sociable, blue-blooded oung gals (and some not *quite* so blue-blooded, like Nigella Lawson) adept at organizing publicity. At one point Rebecca Fraser, daughter of that incomparable pearl the Lady Antonia who used to perform a similar function for George Weiden-

feld twenty years ago), was arranging all the publishing par
ties, at which Naim wanders about displaying the engagin
propensity to assume that everyone he meets has in him
project worth backing.

Naim doesn't just mix art, politics and business together
he combines everything; but the muddle is clarified by a sens
of purpose and efficiency which is almost Napoleonic. He i
endearing, funny and self-mocking. If he can get hold of
and keep, a good editor, then Quartet could, as they claim
'seriously affect our habits'.

Some of our habits have already been affected by a recen
change in attitudes which has enabled new specialist firms t
appear on the publishing scene for the first time.

As a corollary to the success of the Women's Movement
Virago and other feminist publishers have sprung wells o
companionship and profit. The Gay Movement ditto.

Brilliance Books is run by Tenebris Light assisted by Ro
Trevelion and Jeanette Winterson. They reproduced six title
last year including Gertrude Stein's *Paris France* and Jea
Cocteau's autobiography. Gay Men's Press have over twent
titles in print specifically aimed at gay male readers, and od
ones like Peter Tatchell's *The Battle for Bermondsey*.

General publishers also produce books on homosexua
themes of course. Penguin published to scathing reviews thei
*Book of Homosexual Verse*, Faber brought out Adam Mars
Jones's anthology of gay short stories, *Mae West is Dead*, an
Picador published *A Boy's Own Story* by Edmund Whit
(who claimed, in a gay newspaper, to have slept with fiftee
hundred men before he was fifteen). Turned down initially b
Deutsch, Cape, Macmillan and a host of others, Edmun
White's story was finally taken by Sonny Mehta for Picador
Is this a portent? Certainly *A Boy's Own Story* has been
great success.

Sonny Mehta frequently commissions paperback original
with great success. He is a powerful exponent of marketing.

My job is to be enthusiastic, to sell, market and promot
with enthusiasm, to make it impossible for literary editor

and feature writers to ignore my books. I send out personal copies, have brochures printed, dump bins and posters. I talk to people. You can't assume people will notice a book: my job is to make it as difficult as possible for them to ignore it. If you don't promote a book it will remain low profile. A publisher's job is to do the very best he can to market the book well.

onny Mehta has certainly proved his ability, not only with dmund White's work but also with *The Female Eunuch* by ermaine Greer and *Dispatches* by Michael Herr.

Publishing needs no qualifications and therefore cannot chnically be regarded as a profession. Nor is it necessarily n occupation for gentlemen', the title suggested by the late ord Sieff to the late Fredric Warburg for his autobiography. leither is it a closed shop. When he was a student in a olytechnic in the Tottenham Court Road, Ernest Hecht ought, for £60 advance from the agent Rosica Colin, the ublication rights of a book, long buried in the pre-war file opies of Laffont in Paris, about elephants. The magazine ghts he had already sold in France and Germany. Hecht had o capital – his father did the packing – was a Jewish refugee nd had few connections. Anyone can set up in publishing ny time, any place; some of those who begin in a small way ay small, and the classic imprint in this field is that of Peter wen.

eter Owen founded his house in 1951 with, as he says, nthusiasm but no great conviction of success on a capital of ss than £1,000'.

Publishing pundits at the time predicted that it would be impossible to succeed without a capital of £250,000 and today I would consider that a minimum of a million pounds would be needed. Even that sum could easily be lost if not administered by a competent publisher. Furthermore, both then and now, the greatest care is needed to avoid unnecessary overheads, overprinting, and, initially, binding too

many books, and to buy printing and paper at the mos
favourable prices.

My first list included some distinguished but unfashior
able authors – Hermann Hesse (who accepted an advanc
of £25 for *Siddhartha*, later to become an international cu
bestseller), Henry Miller's *The Books in My Life*, Ezr
Pound's critical books, *Guide to Kulchur* and his *Spirit c
Romance* – as well as an anthology of 'modern' Russia
literature, two novels by French writers and William Carlo
Williams's epic poem *Paterson*, which was later remair
dered.

The intention was to endeavour to produce a consistentl
'literary' list, in relatively small printings. At that time
was easier to sell books to the public and lending librarie
and to overseas markets. Prices of hardbacks were infinitel
cheaper than now. Our prices were usually higher tha
other publishers', because of the nature of the books. Unt
about three years ago most publishers grossly unde
priced their books, relying on the occasional bestselle
or educational books to subsidize the 'trade' list. Als
until relatively recently, there was over-production, an
many books, particularly novels, should never have bee
published.

In my initial enthusiasm, having read the manuscript o
the translation of *Siddhartha*, given to me by a kindl
American publisher, I could not wait for my compan
stationery to be printed; I wrote to Hermann Hesse on m
own writing paper. The reply from Frau Hesse was prompt
they did not deal with unknown publishers. Feeling s
strongly about the book, I was determined to publish i
and as my father and uncle were also running a publishin
firm, I asked them to bid for it. Their offer was promptl
accepted and this and other Hesse books for a time appeare
under the joint imprint Peter Owen/Vision Press. Eventu
ally, when Vision Press was sold, I bought them out
subsequently the books all became hardback and paperbac
bestsellers.

My first editor, after three years, was Muriel Spark, wh
had just completed her first novel, and was pessimisticall

awaiting its publication. She was very efficient, and her salary for three days' work a week was £5. We published two of her earlier non-fiction books, *The Letters of John Henry Newman* and *Emily Brontë*, now in its fifth printing. After the success of Muriel's *The Comforters* she decided to write full time. Her successor, who remained with me for some years, was another writer, Elizabeth Berridge.

Money was very tight, and every book had to be budgeted. I had the choice of publishing a distinguished Japanese author, Osamu Dazai, or Samuel Beckett's *Murphy*. I mistakenly chose Dazai's *The Setting Sun* (distinguished, translated by *the* authority Donald Keene, but even now still in its first edition). We could not afford to do Beckett as well, not realizing that in his middle age he was destined for international fame. One of my errors!

Gradually, as the backlist built up, there was a financial easing, although the first eight or ten years continued to require great care and hard work, much of it routine. I had been trained in book production, and for the first three years both edited and designed my books. I believe it is essential for a successful publisher to know every aspect of the profession.

We have published many well-known and distinguished writers and books, such as Erté's autobiography, *Things I Remember*, Dame Edith Sitwell, Boris Pasternak, the novels of Pavese and a number of books by Colette. Having published an esoteric earlier novel by Violette Leduc, we subsequently acquired her bestseller, *La Bâtarde*.

One of my writers, Margaret Crosland, reminded me that Salvador Dali had written a brilliant novel, *Hidden Faces*. I wrote several letters without reply, then met Dali in Paris, and he suggested I visit him at his summer house in Spain. It appeared that *Hidden Faces* had only been published in the US and UK in the 1940s and had never been translated or reprinted. Dali's price was steep, £5,000, which was a lot ten years ago, and he offered to do some new drawings to 'sweeten' the pill. I considered I had grossly overpaid, until I started selling foreign editions. The publishers were vying to buy the rights in the novel, and we easily retrieved the initial investment. Dali, who could be very practical, had informed me that the US rights had never been reverted. The editor for the original US publisher came up to me at the Frankfurt Book Fair, where *Hidden Faces* was 'the book of the fair', and asked if the rights were free! My reply was that for 'technical' reasons we were not offering it in the US at present, but would certainly bear their interest in mind. They discovered, when they returned to New York, that they owned the rights. They could have reprinted or even photostated a few copies to retain copyright. But after an initial lawyer's letter it was forgotten, and we sent them a letter of rights reversion, and after the time-limit expiry sold it quietly to another American publisher. I always found Dali approachable and helpful, but when visiting him always took a present or some money on account of his royalties. He signed copies of the German and English limited editions which appeared in conjunction with the 'trade' edition.

As to the future, publishers must become more professional and pursue every avenue of sales, and make their books look more attractive with first-class cover designs. Packaging is as important in books as in other commodities. Public library allocations have been savagely cut in the past years, both here and abroad, and a lot more money needs to be injected, as the bulk of sales, especially of fiction, is to libraries. More subsidies are required both here and from foreign governments to make available the best English and international literature, which with lesser-known writers publishers are no longer able to finance, with falling sales, increasing costs, and expensive translations. The alternative would be cultural stagnation and the eventual phasing out of new writers, who stand little chance of publication at present. In the non-fiction field, a similar reluctance to publish the unusual, the provocative or the controversial, in my opinion, would be a disaster.

With an eye to future trends, we have recently started a US subsidiary which will enable us to publish books not taken up by American trade houses. Such distinguished writers as Peter Vansittart, whose books we publish successfully in the British Commonwealth market, can in this way be introduced to Americans. As with our English programme, it will be a pioneering list.

The annual award of the Booker Prize regularly generates a furore over the ethics of publishers. They are accused of exploiting their authors and debasing literature. Fay Weldon, in an attack in *The Times*, even complained that they profit from sales of books by dead authors. So they do – and so do dead authors' estates. As readers of this will know by now, copyright obtains for fifty years after the death of the author. (This is good news for any agent representing a recently deceased at eighty-odd and prolific author, like Somerset Maugham, who had four plays running in the West End in 1908, which means that if they were revived in 2008 royalties would still be payable.)

Publishers do indeed appear to enjoy a fuller life style than *most* of their authors, but the really successful writers, like Harold Robbins and Jeffrey Archer, earn a great deal more than any of their publishers. Trade or general publishers, as opposed to textbook publishers who *really* earn money and carry on like undertakers, are indeed relentless party-givers and heavy lunchers, but that is the nature of the animal. Further, we seek publicity because our business is to make things public.

The detractors of publishers never reckon the money which is written off in advances which are unearned, or for books which are never delivered, nor the conscious decision made to publish by a group of human beings supposedly commercially oriented, on the grounds of 'we don't care if this book does not make money, but it absolutely has to see the light of day'. There cannot be many industries in which this argument has finality.

It would be repetitive to continue describing publishers I know or have met, but I hope I have given enough details to show their range and versatility, their powerful individuality and their receptiveness to new ideas. Although I have made much of the tycoon aspect of publishing in this chapter, success lies in excellent teamwork: the big names would get nowhere without their editors, production departments, designers, publicists and sales representatives, all of whom play their part and all of whom are dealt with more fully later on in this book. Now follows a brief list of some of the smaller publishing houses with a further list of various other imprints belonging to larger firms in alphabetical order with a pertinent few lines about each. Again, I must reiterate that many more firms are mentioned in the *Writers' and Artists' Yearbook* published by A. & C. Black at £4.50. There is also a guide to *The Small Publisher* compiled and published by Audrey and Philip Ward and available from 17 Stansgate Avenue, Cambridge.

## *Small Publishers*

AIDAN ELLIS PUBLISHING
Cobb House, Nuffield, Henley-on-Thames, Oxon
A bright, I suspect rather rich, young man whose books have a businesslike mainstream feeling. Very keen on Henri Troyat.

CARCANET NEW PRESS LTD
208 Corn Exchange Buildings, Manchester
Michael Schmidt, a novelist in his own right, runs the editorial side. Carcanet differs from other small presses in its commitment to the wide field of literature. Though its primary concern is poetry, its growing list includes fiction, criticism and memoirs. It insists on its freedom within the 'Imaginary Museum' and publishes both English and translated poetry and fiction from various periods, being Anglo-European rather than Anglo-American in bias. Publishes distinguished senior British writers and some of the best of modern Europe including Milosz, Pasolini and Robert Walser. Carcanet has recently been bought by Bob Gavron.

J. L. CARR
27 Milldale Road, Kettering, Northants
In 1964 Mr Carr produced a sixteen-page booklet of John Clare's poems, price sixpence to adults and fourpence to children. After a mention in the *Guardian* 'letters came tied

in bundles. I lost a penny on each book thanks to the enormous number of children with thoroughly mature handwriting.' He publishes one-page architectural/historical English county maps, and tiny books such as Carr's *Dictionary of Extraordinary English Cricketers* (35p) which has sold over 20,000 copies.

CENTAUR PRESS LTD
Fontwell, Arundel, Sussex
English literary classics. Jon Wynne-Tyson started by impressing printers in a borrowed Rolls-Royce. He used to have reps but no longer bothers. 'The outlook for small publishers in general is very good if they ignore the "mystique" put about by their elders and study what people want to read by observing people and not urban trendies in Mayfair pubs.' (Mr Jon Wynne-Tyson is wrong about location. Bloomsbury or Soho would be more accurate.)

FINDHORN PUBLICATIONS
The Park, Forres, Scotland
Publishes books from messages received from another world: also latterday Patience Strongs. *God Spoke Unto Me* has sold over 15,000 copies.

GABERBOCCHUS PRESS
42a Formosa Street, London W9
Zany, surreal little books with titles like *Ubu Roi*, *The Good Citizen's Alphabet*, *Professor Mmaa's Lecture* and *Cardinal Polatuo*. Run by the Polish poets Stefan and Franciszka Themerson.

THE HARVESTER PRESS
16 Ship Street, Brighton, Sussex
John Spiers, the owner-driver, is one of the few publishers with a Rolls-Royce. He specializes in recondite monographs for American University Presses, who are good payers, and his positive cash flow allows him to be fierce with printers. Harvester published Douglas Hofstadler's *Godel, Escher, Bach*.

C. HURST & CO. LTD
38 King Street, London WC2
Had a presence at the Frankfurt Book Fair and the Association of American University Presses Conference but it is the smallest publisher we know, with a workforce of two and a steady output since 1967 of twelve titles a year. The books are sturdy, plain and necessarily expensive, but some people have to know about *Antarctic Law* and the history of relatively arcane areas in Venezuela. He says 'authors and publishers are spread thinly world wide.' He says also that he is in business for the good of his health and enjoys every moment of it, as well as earning a living.

MICHAEL RUSSELL
The Chantry, Wilton, Salisbury
Publishes from the dining-room table. Produced delightful small book by Paul Theroux with drawings by Patrick Procktor, entitled *Sailing Through China*.

THE STOURTON PRESS
18 Royal Crescent, London W11 4SL
*Belles Lettres* around octogenarians like Dadie Rylands and John Piper, as elegant and well-bred as the sole prop. the Hon. James Stourton, a perfect example of a dining room and garage publisher.

COLIN SMYTHE LTD
PO Box 6, Gerrards Cross, Bucks
Colin Smythe founded his own publishing house on leaving Trinity College Dublin in 1966. It is totally a one-man show. Fifty per cent of his titles are commissioned and 50 per cent unsolicited. 'Most of our authors are dead, so it is a matter of ascertaining scholarly needs.'

BARBARA WOODHOUSE
Campions, Croxley Green, Rickmansworth, Herts
No hope here for unsolicited manuscripts: Mrs Woodhouse publishes and distributes the animal books that *she* writes. Her two bestsellers are *The Book of Ponies* (74,000) and *Dog Training My Way* (53,000).

## *Larger hardback publishing houses*

This list is intended to give the flavour of the varied imprints to help aspiring writers choose a likely home. Some of these hardback houses also publish paperbacks. Upmarket literary products, for instance, should be shown to the likes of Cape, Chatto, Faber and, dare I say it, Anthony Blond, and not to John Boon of Mills & Boon whose blue Rolls-Royce (his brother has a Panther) is often parked outside the Garrick, a testimony to the fact that light romance sells better.

(GEORGE) ALLEN & UNWIN PUBLISHERS LTD
Ruskin House, 40 Museum Street, London WC1
August, independent family affair, specializing in tertiary education and occasionally lashing out with a big non-fiction title. Two sets of management accounts are kept, one with, and one without, sales of Tolkien.

About 130 staff, including warehouse, home sales force, etc. About 200 titles per annum. Every contracted author must be the publisher's favourite. Historically the longest and happiest relationship has been with J. R. R. Tolkien and his heirs. 'Every manuscript received is considered seriously and expectantly at senior editorial level.' They say.

ALLISON & BUSBY LTD
6A Noel Street, London W1
Clive Allison (pale) and Margaret Busby (dark) plough a brave little furrow in the DIY area of publishing. They occasionally have hits like *The Spook Who Sat by the Door*, *Book of Five Rings* and Anthony Burgess's *Ninety-nine Novels*. They have excellent taste and, rare birds, enjoy the protection of Richard Hoare of the equally special Bank of C. Hoare & Co.

ASSOCIATED BOOK PUBLISHERS (UK) LTD
11 New Fetter Lane, London EC4
(ABP) This is the largest congeneracy, to use a dreadful word invented by Mr Hegel of Macmillan, New York. It includes

Eyre & Spottiswoode, which, although owned by a Catholic family – the Crosthwaite Eyres – is licensed to publish the Authorized Version of the Bible, and Methuen, who reprint *Winnie the Pooh* in swathes of 50,000. They are good at plays, e.g. Harold Pinter's *The Caretaker*. They are presided over by Michael Turner. Employees in the UK publishing 390, total worldwide, just over 1,000. Active titles on UK list about 6,000. New books and new editions published by the UK companies in 1981 total 758. Bestsellers in all categories and they range from *Winnie the Pooh*, *The Secret Diary of Adrian Mole Age 13¾* to *The Supreme Court Practice*. Manuscripts are welcomed provided they are in readable form.

BASIL BLACKWELL, PUBLISHERS, LTD
108 Cowley Road, Oxford
Better known as the Oxford booksellers with the most distinguished and profitable export mailing list in the world (from former undergraduates who are now African dictators). From the same source this imprint captures bright young dons. Sir Basil was a wily old bird who, aged eighty, claimed he had been 'scarred for life' by reading *Last Exit to Brooklyn*. Sir John (Bruno) Brown (q.v.), formerly publisher to the University Press (OUP), was chairman.

THE BODLEY HEAD LTD
30 Bedford Square, London WC1B 3EL
Founded by John Lane in 1887, uncle of Sir Allen Lane. A motley collection of imprints dominated by the wise and lucky, night and day owl, Max Reinhardt, who is, with Graham C. Greene, co-chairman of the Chatto, Virago, Bodley Head & Cape Ltd group and a major shareholder. One of his directors was the late Sir Ralph Richardson, who, through his friendship with the banker George Ansley, more or less presented Max with the Bodley Head on a plate. Imprints include the defunct Hollis and Carter, Putnam & Co. Ltd, T. Werner Laurie Ltd, all famous in the 1930s. They also own the Nonesuch Library and re-started the Nonesuch Press with Sir Frances Meynell in 1953, reprinting rare and

lovely classics. Their prize author is Graham Greene, whose latest book *The Tenth Man* has recently been co-published with Anthony Blond. They also publish William Trevor and Muriel Spark and a very fine list of children's books. David Machin stopped running The Society of Authors to become Managing Director in 1981 and, as we go to press, a new Publishing Director, Chris Holifield, formerly of Sphere, has been appointed.

MARION BOYARS, PUBLISHERS, LTD
18 Brewer Street, London W1
Once allied to John Calder; her offices in Soho conceal a telephone that no one can ever find. Specialists in exotic Balkaniana. Indefatigable and chaotic. Three in-house employees. Twenty-five titles a year. 'Too many authors to list and it would be unfair to list favourites for publication.' On principle they do not accept unsolicited manuscripts, yet when they appear interesting they look at them. However, out of about 10,000 submitted over fifteen years they have taken only three! (This is slightly lower than the Anglo-American average – about .05 per cent for acceptance of unsolicited manuscripts.)

JONATHAN CAPE LTD
32 Bedford Square, London WC1B 3EL
Originally founded by Herbert J. Cape who was Duckworth's manager. Gerald Duckworth 'did not regard him as a social equal' so would not make him a director (from the official biography). His first book (a reprint) was C. M. Doughty's *Travels in Arabia Deserta* and is still in print. Liz Calder is *the* editor here. Tom Maschler is the Chairman with Graham C. Greene managing. (Graham C. Greene is chairman of the group holding company.) Tom, who has done more than anyone in London to promote literary prizes, is adventurous, publicity-conscious and still fizzy. Cape's have 40 in-house employees and publish approximately 100 titles a year; their newest fiction authors include, Anita Brookner, Lisa St Aubin de Terán, Salman Rushdie, Ian McEwan, John Irving, Martin Amis, Julian Barnes, Christopher Priest, Ahdaf Soueif, Paul

Bailey, Bernard Mac Laverty, Janet Hobhouse and Deborah Moggach. At least one person reads everything that comes in to their office whether solicited or not. They would naturally prefer to receive an explanatory letter in advance but, they are 'ever full of hope'.

CHATTO & WINDUS
40 William IV Street, London WC2
Virago, Chatto & Windus and The Hogarth Press are all at the same address but are absolutely separate companies under the Chatto, Virago, Bodley Head and Jonathan Cape Ltd umbrella. Chatto & Windus, a cool classy imprint where the feminist publisher Carmen Callil (q.v.) is the big vegetable. Twenty-six employees and the number of titles for the year was 80 with 29 reissues. Some of the newest authors are Christopher Simon Sykes, Caroline Davidson, Maggie Brooks, Angela Carter, Richard Cobb, Michael Ignatieff and Snoo Wilson. Again their attitude to unsolicited manuscripts is benevolent.

VIRAGO PRESS, the original feminist success, was founded in 1972 by Carmen Callil with three colleagues. The obvious first base for a non-male person's literary efforts. In-house employees were 15 and they published 70 new titles and 4 reissues. Recent authors are Pat Barker, Barbara Taylor and Christa Wolf and they again have a benevolent attitude to unsolicited manuscripts.

WILLIAM COLLINS, SONS & CO. LTD
8 Grafton Street, London W1
Recently rocked by a family rift and takeover threats, is now back on course with a spread of imprints – Collins, Willow & Harvill as well as the paperback Fontana – under the cunning helmsman Ian Chapman as a flagship of British trade publishing. Roger Schlesinger is editor-in-chief. Collins now owns Granada too. An excellent place to train in. Christopher Maclehose now runs The Harvill Press, a tiny subsidiary which nevertheless, under Manya Harari, published *Dr Zhivago*, *The Leopard* and *Born Free*.

GERALD DUCKWORTH & CO. LTD
The Old Piano Factory, 43 Gloucester Crescent, London NW1
Colin Haycraft is Chairman and Managing Director. The Old Piano Factory they inhabit includes a computer which, to quote the scholarly proprietor, 'can't ask for a rise'. Has titles like *The Greek Homosexuality 1978*, 244pp, only £15. Originally published Caroline Blackwood, possibly the sharpest pen in the kingdom. Some authors leave in despair at the high prices placed upon their wares. Published the only book with no colour on Turkish carpets. They have 12 in-house employees and the latest number of titles is 50. Among the favourite and newest authors are Beryl Bainbridge, Hugh Lloyd-Jones, G. E. M. de Ste Croix, R. L. Gregory and Hilaire Belloc. This house welcomes unsolicited manuscripts.

ANDRÉ DEUTSCH LTD
105 Great Russell Street, London WC1
Tom Rosenthal, blocked from the throne at Heinemann, has joined forces with André. Strong journalistic connections (the Insight team) guarantee hard-nosed ephemera, e.g. *The Falklands War*. Good children's and fiction lists. In-house employees total 36 and 2 part-timers. They publish 71 titles a year. Their authors include Peter Benchley, Geoffrey Hill, Molly Keane, Laurie Lee, George Mikes, Timothy Mo, V. S. Naipaul, the late Ogden Nash and John Updike along with Celia Berridge, John Cunliffe, Mary Melwood and Jan Needle from the children's list. They do read unsolicited manuscripts, every one is looked at and discussed at length at editorial meetings and then most of them are rejected.

FABER & FABER LTD
3 Queen Square, London WC1
One of the first hardback publishers to do their own quality paperback. Upmarket non-fiction of an arty kind with a cosy medical line. Publishers of T. S. Eliot, who was a director. They employ 104 staff including those at their warehouse in Harlow. They publish about 190 books per annum including various new editions. Faber has many distinguished deceased writers but among the living authors they publish are Philip Larkin,

Lawrence Durrell, William Golding, P. D. James, Ted Hughes, Seamus Heaney, Tom Stoppard, David Hare, Christopher Hampton and George Steiner. Amongst their list of newest authors they include: Peter Carey, Adam Mars-Jones, Kazuo Ishiguro, Milan Kundera, Mario Vargas Llosa, Woody Allen and Andrea Lee. Faber read all unsolicited manuscripts very carefully, their list is wide-ranging.

VICTOR GOLLANCZ LTD
14 Henrietta Street, London WC2
Victor's daughter Livia continues the tradition of fine and courteous publishing; though less egocentric and left-wing than in dad's day. Famous for crime and science fiction but an all round imprint, meticulous and beloved by the trade. The in-house employees total 56 and they have 145 titles; among their newest and most recently published authors are: Muriel Box, Alec Clifton-Taylor, Polly Devlin, David Gethin, Hubert Gregg, Torey Hayden, Lucy Irvine, Susan Lasdun, Robin Lloyd-Jones, Helen Muir, Peter Padfield, Brough Scott, Katie Stewart and Andrew Taylor. All manuscripts are looked at, but they prefer a synopsis and specimen chapter in the first instance.

HAMISH HAMILTON LTD
Garden House, 57 Long Acre, London WC2
The founder Hamish ('Jamie') Hamilton, still incredibly a commoner, is still with us but mainly in Italy so the firm is run by Christopher Sinclair-Stevenson, an orthodox man of whom only kind words are spoken. Although owned by the Thomson Organization is still a distinguished imprint. Publishes Nancy Mitford and Raymond Briggs. Their in-house employees total 54. Number of titles in print is approximately 920 of which 400 are general books, 410 children's books and 110 Elm Tree which are specialized subjects and entertainments. The number of titles published in 1982 were general 86, children's 78 and Elm Tree 28. They have a large list of favourite authors which includes Edward Blishen, Philip Howard, Susan Hill, Robert McCrum, Paul Theroux, William Boyd, Jane Gardam, Jennifer Johnston, Miles Kington and many others. Their newest authors include Clare Boylan,

Stephen Vizinczey, Nikolai Tolstoy, Peter Ackroyd and Robert Elegant, to name but a few. Unsolicited manuscripts are entirely welcome, all are read and all reacted to.

WILLIAM HEINEMANN LTD
10 Upper Grosvenor Street, London W1
The original Mr Heinemann wrapped tracts round little packets of tea for sale to those who couldn't afford to buy by the pound. Now they cover the field and have a huge educational list lightened by the Made Simple series they bought from W. H. Allen. Original publishers of Graham Greene and W. Somerset Maugham. A big affair once owned by Thomas Tilling, the haulage contractors, who bought it out of their nationalization pay-off, now taken over by BTR. Dominated by Charles Pick and, until 1984, fleshed out by polymathrabbinical Tom Rosenthal. They also own the more literary and exotic Secker & Warburg which has a branch line in Leo Cooper who publishes military history, like Brig. Julian Thompson's ('Thomp the Yomp') book on the Falklands assisted by a scrum of apprentices from his old school, Radley. A big chunk of their business is from Heinemann Educational, which is powerful in West Africa.

HODDER & STOUGHTON LTD
47 Bedford Square, London WC1
This family firm also runs two paperback lines, Coronet and the recently acquired New English Library as well as Educational and Children's Companies. Formerly middle brow/road, Hodders have gone all out for blockbusters. Slightly restrained by the presence of a profitable religious list. Philip Attenborough (Chairman) and Michael Attenborough (group Managing Director) preside whilst Eric Major manages the hardback side, ably backed by Ion Trewin. They own the *Lancet*. They employ 474 in-house staff in the UK, which includes 147 editorial, publicity, rights and production, 90 sales personnel and 237 people in administration, accounts and distribution. The titles are 7,500 and among their authors are John Le Carré, James Clavell, Jeffrey Archer, Morris West, Gavin Lyall and Fay Weldon, to name a few.

The NEW ENGLISH LIBRARY, which is part of the Hodder & Stoughton Group, functions quite separately. Although the do not disclose their turnover and profit, they admit that th latter is looking quite healthy. Their in-house employees tota 16 and other personnel are shared with the Group. The publish approximately 135 new paperback titles per annun and 40–45 new hardcover titles and library reprints are alway coming in and out of the inventory. All their authors ar equally cherished. Their attitude to unsolicited manuscript is probably shared by most publishers, it is a mixture o sympathy and depression. All manuscripts are looked at care fully and the more promising ones usually have a detailec reader's report. They are keen to buy new talent in principl but a depressingly small proportion is good and the attitud of the book trade towards unknown writers makes judgmen rigorous.

MICHAEL JOSEPH LTD
44 Bedford Square, London WC1
Possibly the most consistently successful imprint (they pub lished *Country Diary of an Edwardian Lady*) since its foun dation in 1935. Michael Joseph himself liked cats, once mar ried Hermione Gingold, and supported Victor Gollancz. Wit safe bestsellers like James Herriot, Dick Francis, Monic Dickens, Paul Gallico, Miss Read, H. E. Bates and Sta Barstow, to name but a few. A bit of gloss is added b Alan Brooke, the Managing Director and Philippa Harriso (ex-Cape, ex-Hutchinson) is among London's powerful pub lishers. They employ a staff of 70 in-house. Their titles ar approximately 144 including Pelham and various joint im prints but excluding Ebury Press distribution. Recent author include Sally Emerson, Bryan Forbes, Irving Wallace, Ma Hastings, but there are many others. All manuscripts ar considered, however briefly; they prefer sample copy at firs rather than the entire manuscript.

MACMILLAN LTD
4 Little Essex Street, London WC2
Alan Maclean, whom Harold Macmillan appointed in com pensation for having to leave the Foreign Office, was Chair

nan until Julian Ashby took over in 1983. Still a distinguished mprint (though made a bit of a boo boo over the new *Grove's )ictionary of Music*). A fine spot for an elegant first novel. /ery powerful in the Third World. The following details do ıot relate to the entire Macmillan Group owned by Macmillan 'ublishers but refer only to their General Publishing com- ›anies, i.e. Macmillan London Ltd, Papermac and Macmillan ;hildren's Books. There are 40 employees, excluding 14 reps. 'itles are: Macmillan London 50 fiction and 45 non-fiction; 'apermac 60 non-fiction; Macmillan Children's Books 40 ıovelty and fiction and 20 non-fiction. Among new authors re Peter Ustinov, Greg Matthews, Mary Wesley, Larry Gray- on, Ronald Searle and David Irving. They receive approxi- nately 2,000 unsolicited manuscripts each year and all are ead.

ɪITCHELL BEAZLEY LTD
Mill House, 87 Shaftesbury Avenue, London W1
)riginal part-work publishers. International wheeler-dealers, xcellent guide books. Very modern, into video, were once a ubsidiary of American Express. International reference books nd encyclopaedias. At present employ around 120 people. 'here are approximately 150 titles on their list, growing ɔ about 200 over the next eighteen months. Their best- elling authors have been Hugh Johnson with his *World ıtlas of Wine*, Alex Comfort and his *The Joy of Sex*, Terence ;onran with his *House Book* and Patrick Moore with ıis many astronomy books. Their biggest project is an ncyclopaedia – *The Joy of Knowledge* – with contributions rom about 250 authors, consistently updated in 27 editions ı 22 languages. They would like to receive more manuscripts han they do, since they are always in dread of running out f ideas.

OHN MURRAY LTD
0 Albemarle Street, London W1
ince 1768 publishers of poets from Byron to Betjeman. John Jock) Murray is your classic English publisher, but Kenneth 'innock's schoolbooks made the money. Staff is approxi- nately 80 including warehouse and distribution personnel.

Titles between 80 and 90. Some authors are John Betjeman Meira Chand, Kenneth Clark, Ruth Prawer Jhabvala, Patric Leigh-Fermor and Freya Stark. All manuscripts are welcome – 'swans sail in among the geese'.

THAMES & HUDSON LTD
30 Bloomsbury Street, London WC1
Now the leaders in art books but with the addition of brillian and popular Nikos Stangos willing to try anything beyon those frontiers. They also publish archaeology, architecture travel, history and science. Owned by the Neurath family Used to employ the Hon. Simon Marks but he became s enraged with one of the sub-editors that he tore off a doo handle and threw it at him.

GEORGE WEIDENFELD & NICOLSON LTD
91 Clapham High Street, London SW4
After various ups and ups, now an established imprint whic garners more column inches in the posh papers than an other. Top-level Establishment stuff like *Mountbatten: Her of Our Time* by Richard Hough. Nabokov is one of thei authors, but so are Henry Root and Frances Donaldson. A aspiring author is unlikely to bump into George Weidenfel (q.v.) at one of his parties without going home with th promise of a contract. They have between 80 and 90 in-hous employees and eight full-time travellers. 160–180 titles pe year. Among the substantial list of authors who have pub lished throughout their career and started with Weidenfel are: Antonia Fraser, Elizabeth Longford, Thomas Pakenham Margaret Drabble, Anthony Holden, Peter Bauer, Eri Hobsbawm, Victoria Glendinning and Henry Kissinger. Th latest crop of talented writers includes Marina Warner, Ji Spalding, Hugo Vickers, Adam Nicolson and David Gentle man. Unsolicited manuscripts are seriously sampled. Mar garet Drabble's first novel came 'out of the blue'.

Publishers are properly jealous of their finds. In this book I go on, and will do so to my dyin day, about *Small is Beautiful* by E. F. Schumacher. Fair's fair, and Barley Alison (q.v.), no with Secker and Warburg, claims to have netted Saul Bellow when she was with Weidenfel Similarly, and also in this chapter, Ken Banerji (q.v.) and William Miller (q.v.) point out tha Virago was founded under the umbrella and with the finance of Quartet at a time whe Carmen Callil was successfully publicising that company.

# IV *Approaches*

The acceptance rate of unsolicited manuscripts is about one in every two thousand submitted. This figure obtains on both sides of the Atlantic and has been static for years. Publishers are not infallible and legends of how international bestsellers like *Gone With the Wind* were turned down are true and will continue to be. It is said that W. E. Owen received 173 rejection slips and was never published but that Steven Goldberg's *Inevitability of Patriarchy* was published by the fifty-sixth publisher after it had received sixty-nine rejections. (Cape is one of the few who keep a record of whether or not a manuscript has been sent in previously for consideration.) Sadly most manuscripts or typescripts, to acknowledge their more usual form, are illiterate, and more satisfying for the writer than for the reader. Of the saying that everybody has a book in them, Somerset Maugham commented, 'Yes, but not necessarily a good book.' Doubleday & Co. of New York must lose very little by returning unsolicited manuscripts unopened to the sender and they will certainly save themselves a great deal of postage. Heaven is a place where there are no rejection slips; while on earth an author must stir himself mightily.

A writer does himself a great disservice if his manuscript is not typed on one side of the paper only, double-spaced, reasonably pristine and held together in some fashion. Pity the poor reader when the sheets fall all over the place as in a

Buster Keaton sketch. Make sure that the manuscript is legible throughout and is not so faint on some pages that the text cannot be deciphered. Retyped manuscripts need final checking; even the most devoted Mummy or girlfriend may let her eyes leapfrog. I often feel like founding a society for providing indigent authors with new typewriter ribbons. Despite the eye-strain there is a strange benefit to be gained by struggling through unpublished manuscripts: one gains such esoteric information, for example, as that there are forty thousand people of Cornish extraction living in the Bronx.

Would-be writers are warned against word processors. These should be manipulated only by exceptionally skilled professionals or those whose style is already terse, for they encourage garrulity. Putting everything you know, and have learned in the library, between covers, does not make a book. Moreover, word processors make correcting individual paragraphs too easy: the author just revamps a few sentences, presses a button and the ensuing paragraphs roll out. But if you changed the argument in one paragraph, then logically you must continue to change the next ones too, otherwise you will be producing hundreds of random paragraphs, all looking exquisite but making little sense. The day has already arrived when a book can be set for printing from the author's own word processor direct: it was done in the case of Rupert Allason's *The Special Branch*. But ask Barley Alison of Secker & Warburg about the headaches it caused . . .

Assume you have written a thriller, a literary novel, a piece of science fiction, or a non-fiction adventure story. Most books fall into *some* sort of category, although a few, like the *Confessions of Zeno* by Italo Svevo – a masterpiece which took twenty-six years to get published in England – and *Schindler's Ark* by Thomas Keneally, gained from not being easily labelled. Turn now to the list of selected literary agents at the end of Chapter II or the list of publishers at the end of Chapter III and see where your work might fit in. Buy, borrow and study books on a theme close to your own. Approach the relevant publisher.

Write a letter which begins with a paragraph about yourself; then explain in quick outline what you have written, giving its approximate length, whether fiction or non-fiction. Follow this up with a third paragraph saying that you would like to submit this manuscript for consideration because you have been greatly impressed by one of the books they have (handled if a literary agent) published recently; then name it. Do not send the manuscript with the letter but wait until you have received an answer.

When you do send the manuscript in, be sure to check that you have written your name and address on the outer cover of the manuscript and on the title page. Send stamps to cover return postage. Most publishers state clearly in print at the bottom of their writing paper that although they take every care, they are not responsible for its loss. Be warned.

Publishers should acknowledge receipt of your offering with a printed form. Time will pass; it could be a good sign. After six weeks (I am sorry) a polite letter from you is in order. Another fortnight and you can be more fierce. It is inadvisable to wait anxiously for three and a half years as happened to an author quoted in *The Times* of January 1st, 1984, for he never saw his manuscript again. Most of the agony in submitting to publishers can be relieved if you are accepted as a client by some literary agent, which professional publishers regard as a filter, and whose submissions are treated more seriously. But I cannot repeat often enough, it is rare for a book to be accepted by a publisher out of the blue; the odds are 2,000 to 1.

A submarine commander wrote about his Second World War experiences and sent the manuscript to Michael Joseph. The commander received a contract for publication a month later which he obediently signed and returned. Then he got a letter saying the book had been optioned by a movie company, then another saying that the paperback rights had been sold. He thought this was routine for all first books.

As a would-be author, learn how to interpret a rejection letter from a publisher: it may be couched in polite and kindly language but if it says no an author has to learn to accept that the manuscript has been turned down. 'I am sure this book gave more pleasure in the writing than in the reading' is an unkind but truthful form of rejection. One of the toughest things for a publisher or an agent to have to do is to tell someone that they cannot write and should desist forthwith. If he wraps up the truth too much, the author seems never to take it in; if he is too brutally honest, it can be cruel.

Maybe the rejected author needs to go out and live it up a bit more, meet more people, gain experience. ('Give him a thousand dollars a year and tell him to go to hell,' was Somerset Maugham's advice in 1908 to a doting mother about her aspiring author son.) Perhaps the wrong publisher or agent has been approached, perhaps first efforts need scrapping in favour of a new subject. Never mind, writing can be a therapy and a joy in itself. Margaret Drabble regards publication as a bonus.

Paying to get your book into print is neither sinful nor illegal. The collected works of Ivy Compton-Burnett, considered a genius if an acid one, would not be available from Gollancz had she not left money for that purpose. Here, however, is a salutary tale about a fan club that was surely deluded.

Touring the London Book Fair in 1982, I paused at corner stand 211, brightly lit and well furnished. I spotted, with my famous talent-oriented eye, a bottle of gin and some tonic, sat down and introduced myself. The publishers were called Lashbrook & Knight and they had published only one book, *The Quest of Aah* by Alexan Farelane, 616 pp, £7.95. ISBN 09507559 07, set and printed in 11 on 12 point Plantin by Redwood Burn. It looked, for all the world, like any other book on display at the Fair. But when Mr Knight, a pleasant-faced young man in a blue suit, informed me that the publishing firm of Lashbrook & Knight had been formed for the SOLE purpose of publishing *The Quest of Aah* and did not intend to add another title to their list, I felt the matter needed to be further explored.

The story goes like this. A group of twenty-five people knew the late Miss Farelane and were impressed by her talent. They were distressed that her typescript had, after much circulation, failed to attract an offer for publication and decided to pool their savings, from £50 to £500, to form a publishing company to publish the book. Mr Lashbrook, an estate agent in Croydon, where most of the contributors live, designed the jacket, and quite striking it is too, in bright geranium with a pair of antlers stuffed into a Nordic knight's helmet decorated with trefoils. The actual object dominated stand 211. They consulted several books for guidance on how to publish and, I am gratified to report, found my own *The Publishing Game* the most helpful. They printed 700 jackets – the number I suggested – and sent them out to the trade. The subscription was not overwhelming – about 90 out of a print order of 2,500 copies, but it did include 25 copies from W. H. Smith, which shows that somewhere in that formidable and computered institution there beats a human heart. *The Quest of Aah* was published in November last year and so far there have been no reviews though there was a mention of the book's existence on LBC. The cost of the enterprise so far is about £9,000. But the Croydon entrepreneurs remain optimistic, and feel justified in spending £500 on taking a stand for the promotion of their one book.

*The Quest of Aah* is about an ordinary family (gosh they can say that again), who, after lunch on Christmas day in 1970 'left the dinner table and retired to the drawing room to sink into soft armchairs. Everyone felt strangely heavy and unusually idle, and fit only for sitting and going to sleep. Seeing what befell them all later in the day, we shall never be sure whether this acute lassitude was due to the warmth, the wine, both or neither.'

There is no need to paraphrase the blurb; it speaks, if that is the word, for itself, so let us continue.

> Thus begins Alexan Farelane's remarkable odyssey: a family very much of this world, transported into a minutely-observed Otherworld, where they find themselves treated as significantly more than guests. Indeed, their visit has been long-planned and each of them must realise that they once had, and must play again, a crucial role in their elusively familiar surroundings.
>
> Their hosts are an Ancient Irish Order – companions of the Grand Fiana, Knights of Aah – and it soon becomes clear . . .

This is where the fun begins. The Starrs at home – I put that in Thornton Heath – are a fairly ordinary lot, or 'folk' as the late Miss Farelane is so prone to say, right-minded but a shade long-winded as the following snatch of dialogue shows. The parents are discussing the events of the previous year and the young folk have gone up to the attic to star-gaze, only they won't see much because it is snowing.

> 'Here ends another fateful year,' she said simply.
>
> 'Yes' answered John with difficulty, 'but each year seems worse than the one before. I must say this last decade has shown a fixed tendency to disaster: incidents almost unbelievable in nature have succeeded one another so swiftly, one can hardly call them to memory when one wants to.'

But when the Starr family are transported into this Otherworld the nomenclature, if not the adventure, really takes off. The Starrs are often taken on excursions by their knightly friends and they go riding in the countryside 'with many a stop to chat and contemplate'. Here follows a description of a typical outing (on page 561):

> At other times, Fin tAahn, Arg Niss Rahm, Bened Issi El, Fi-On and Tu Ah Ta would go out riding: or Fi-On, Tu Ah Ta, Bened Issi El, Cum Na Norn, Mi Ess El and El Da Ray. Or Fi-On, Tu Ah Ta and Cailte would take Elizabeth, Sheila and Henrietta for long and happy rides to lakes and hills, or to one of Fi-On's many lodges. But most times Fi-On, Tu Ah Ta, Bened Issi El and Fin tAahn rode about together. This was a well-earned rest . . .

Yes.

The above extract is copied exactly as printed, em for en on hard, expensive white paper.

This story surely justifies the life-long habit of publishers of saying, mostly, 'no'.

# V *Editing*

Editors have to be able to spell: publishers can be illiterate. I once made the mistake of congratulating, over lunch, that fickle, cantankerous man, Sir Allen Lane, on a recent Pelican. His eyes glazed and he wandered away from the table. My host, Sir William Emrys Williams, a Penguin director, said 'Now you've upset him. Don't you know he can't read?' Sir Allen changed his mind about everything. The lunch in question was about the possibility of my buying his business – the flea buying the dog. He liked gossip, pretty women, champagne and firing people. Sir Allen was none the less, as Sir Robert Lusty said in his eulogy, truly a Companion of Honour.

Editors should be workhorses with an IQ of 180. Until the hard-hearted and practical 1980s, Oxbridge appointments boards were topped up with applications from graduates for jobs in publishing. Now the short-back-and-sides tendency is for IBM and index-linked pensions but editing, call it profession, trade or vocation, though underpaid, still has appeal.

The job description for a junior editorship in one of the more glamorous publishing houses which is large enough to take on inexperienced personnel, let us say Collins, Heinemann or Macmillan, might – if they are honest – go something like this: Junior assistant editor (the pay is low) required for expanding list for general/trade publisher. (It is in fact contracting but there has been a palace revolution and three editors have walked off in a huff.) He or she should be a university graduate (we prefer Oxford or Cambridge but Durham, Exeter, Sussex or London would do at a pinch). Proficiency in one foreign language will be an asset. (This is quite untrue, British publishers are chauvinistic if only because of the costs of translation.) He or she should be unmarried (late nights in pubs and early mornings meeting authors off the New York plane make poor husbands/wives of young editors. *A fortiori*, publicity ladies must be very unmarried, of strong liver and licentious eye). Immediately available and able to type. (We are short-staffed and even shorter of cash so everyone has to lend a hand and be dogsbody.)

What the advertisement also might add is that the new young editor will be expected to behave both romantically and maternally towards the author, be available at all times of day and night for menial tasks like obliging with a tenner or buying theatre tickets. The legendary Maxwell Perkins, who was editor to Hemingway, Fitzgerald and Thomas Wolfe, didn't get very far with his suggestions for cuts but was venerated for his skill at tracing authors' lost luggage, moving their furniture and advancing them cash. For relief he used to pound away at the piano which is still in working order at Scribner's offices in Fifth Avenue. Thomas Wolfe was famous for the length of his typescripts. It was said that they used to come to Scribner's in a Wells Fargo truck. Maxwell Perkins sent Scott Fitzgerald the proof copy of Wolfe's first novel which was dedicated to himself, asking his most famous protégé for a comment, obviously hoping for a puff. Fitzgerald wasn't much help. 'I thought it fell off a bit after the dedication.'

The notion that an editor merely reads a few manuscripts from the slush pile (called transom in America) and sends the rest lazily out to readers is antique. Today he has to hunt for new ideas and authors, commissioning frantically; with zeal and chutzpah he must hurl himself round the party circuit propositioning all whom he meets. Lord Weidenfeld is adept at this: few sit next to him at dinner without being asked to write their life story. In one day over two encounters, he commissioned this author to write a novel about St Paul, a travel guide to Sri Lanka and a digest of the year 1956.

Ideas for books can be found anywhere. Imagine a young ditor having lunch in a Chelsea restaurant – the real work tarts with the third marc de Bourgogne – when a drunken uwaiti is seen waddling over to a table where two obvious sbians are telling each other's fortunes with a pack of cards. le, supposing them to be playing a game of one-eyed Jack, dvises them accordingly. They resist his blandishments until e pays their bill from a very thick wad of twenty-pound otes. All are last glimpsed entering a cab with him *en route* or the Dorchester.

This true scene might seed ideas for books on fortune elling, Tarot, oil, Arab atrocities, or one dealing with the ffect of the Petro-dollar on English life from real estate values n Regent's Park to the re-introduction of white slavery, via t aeroplanes, to the Gulf. Afire with such thoughts, the xuberant young editor races back to the office only to dis-over that the chairman's wife, an amateur interior decorator, refurbishing the Eaton Square apartment of a Saudi Prince; o the deal is off.

The whizzkid editor of the 1950s who excelled at com-nissioning unknown authors whose works then turned out o be bestsellers was Tom Maschler. Were he not the publisher f this book, he would deserve a profile to himself, from his tart with André Deutsch, through Penguin Books to chairman f Jonathan Cape Ltd, possibly the most influential imprint n the land. Tom's reputation as an editor did not rest on just ne book, he managed to pull off coup after coup, in particular Desmond Morris's *The Naked Ape*, *Catch-22*, *Portnoy's Complaint*, Kit Williams's *Masquerade* and the various illus-rated children's books by John Burningham and Nicola ayley. His contemporaries became so jealous of his abilities n the 1960s that they founded a society designed to lower im nearer to their level, rather as the characters in *Winnie he Pooh* tried to debounce Tigger. The inaugural meeting vas held one wet February evening in a bachelor pad. The roceedings were disrupted by the arrival of a very wet and nraged junior publisher who cried out, as he shook his mbrella, 'You can wrap this show up, I've just met Tom Rosenthal.'

Publishers and authors are barely known by name in thi
country outside their own circles. Tom Maschler is the excep
tion. (In a poll of schoolboys taken by *The Times*, Anthon
Burgess, surely one of the most prolific writers, was though
to be the well-known spy.) But Tom's new brainchild ha
exceeded all expectations. It is not a work of literature, indee
it is hardly a book at all for it consists of more than 10
glue points manufactured by nimble-fingered ladies in th
Colombian Andes: it is a piece of three-dimensional pape
engineering which has swept the world (although the Dea
of Westminster Medical School has pointed out that the aorti
and pulmonary valves open the wrong way – but that is
wee niggle over a great enterprise).

Let Tom Maschler tell the story of how he commissione
and produced *The Human Body* by Jonathan Miller an
David Pelham.

I knew David Pelham slightly but had not seen him for
couple of years when we found ourselves judging the D &
AD awards. As an admirer of his *Kites* book, I asked hi
if he was working on anything else. He said that he wa
and that he would come and see me. He arrived with som
rough sketches, not in pop-up form, for *The Human Bod*
and explained what he had in mind. I realized immediatel
that it was going to be an expensive undertaking, wha
with paying David, a paper-engineer, an author and a
artist but by early 1982 we had agreed terms and Jonatha
Miller had offered to write the text.

At the Bologna Book Fair in 1982, I approached th
Carvajal people whose workers are the world's adepts a
glueing pop-ups, and told them we had a 'million-dolla
idea'. In October 1982 we sent our precious dummy t
Carvajal in Colombia for quotation. This was to be forth
coming in two weeks. We heard nothing and telexed. Sti
nothing. Six weeks later we received a telex saying that th
idea was too complicated and too expensive for them t
quote on and suggesting that we should get in touch wit
Intervisual (the world's leading pop-up packagers in Lo
Angeles). We then negotiated terms with them; it wa

agreed that we would do all the creative work and would thus control all foreign rights.

By the time of the Frankfurt Book Fair in October 1982 we had the dummy and two spreads in colour. With this material we made our first sales and decided on a selling price of $4. In order to protect smaller countries and make publication viable for them, we charged all publishers exactly the same amount no matter how many copies they took. The five American publishers to whom we showed the spreads all wanted it. Irv Goodman of Viking was so enthusiastic that he said he would take 5,000 more than the highest alternative offer. Viking took 65,000 copies. At the Fair we also sold the French rights to Larousse after no fewer than nine directors had visited our stand. And in spite of the fact that they declared that decisions without exception are taken only in Paris! Frank Fehmers bought the Dutch rights (10,000 copies). By the time of the Bologna Book Fair in spring '83 we had sold the rights to most major countries throughout the world and by Frankfurt 1983 these included the Hebrew rights, the Arabic rights, with Iceland, Greece (no less) under serious negotiation.

In spring 1983, once we had dummies, we showed *The Human Body* to a few media people. Peter Jackson, editor of the *Sunday Times* colour supplement, offered to publish a spread on it (which he did in his issue of 25th September). Bernard Clark offered to make it one of three items on the first Bookmark programme. This, by one of those 'magical' coincidences, happened to be transmitted Wednesday, 28th September. The eve of our publication date fixed months before and in total innocence. Breakfast TV wanted Jonathan to appear on publication day. Which he did. We had to give our print order in the spring and we decided on a first print of 100,000 copies. On publication day we had subscribed 60,000 with 40,000 in the warehouse. *That* day we received more than 40,000 orders. People who had ordered six were coming back for 100. And one wholesaler who had ordered 500 came back for 7,000. We decided simply on a rationing system and we did it *pro rata* according to the subscription order. It seemed the only fair way.

On publication day we telexed for a reprint of 100,000 copies as soon as possible. Back came a telex offering 25,000 in February 1984 and further batches of 25,000 in March, April and May. Then began a telephone campaign resulting in an instant reprint, 35,000 copies being flown direct from Colombia, the first of them arriving 5th November. Plus a further 25,000 being flown to Miami with a boat from there arriving 1st December. Meanwhile two days after publication we increased 100,000 to 125,000, the balance of these to arrive on a boat from mid-January to mid-February.

*The Human Body* went immediately to number 1 on every bestseller list. It remained there for many weeks. We had also made a commercial and booked space for it. But we postponed until the New Year. The reviews were universally excellent. The most striking being a massive review by Anthony Burgess in the *Observer*. I think it's safe to say that no pop-up has ever had so much editorial space.

It's also safe to say that we deliberately underpriced *The Human Body* at £7.95, and we did not increase the price on the air-freight copies (the direct ones cost an extra $1.10) but we put up the price on 1st January when the printing price also went up. We made a display unit and we also bought 'page-turners' to loan to shops for their windows.

I would attribute the success of *The Human Body* to the fanaticism that went into its creation. Everybody involved has been a perfectionist and literally thousands of hours have gone into it. Certainly it has been by far the most time-consuming publication I have ever encountered. It's worth adding that beyond its obvious immediate dramatic effect the book has real educational value both for children and adults. We deliberately published it as a 'children's book' because it is possible to go from children to adults but not vice versa. It seems to me that this publication uses pop-up form in the most valid way possible, i.e. we've done something with it which could not be done in a normal book and indeed could not even be done on film.

*The Human Body* story is a very modern example of creative publishing: international, ingenious and locking up a great deal of money. I greatly admire Tom's altruism towards smaller booksellers and publishers in this world of hard-nosed marketing, for it is rare in the minds of other mass manufacturers.

This story not only epitomizes the creative energy shown by an outstanding editor but shows how a clever one knows how to make full use of his firm's high-powered machinery to sell his own good idea. This ability to maximize his own company's co-operation and accelerate all employees into top gear when necessary is vital to good editing. In house, the good editor will fight for an extra large share of the firm's attention and money for his or her title, unfair as this may sometimes seem. This means lobbying the sales department to push up the print run, homing in on the publicity department for an increased budget and, finally, intriguing the reviewers. Since a new book is published every twenty minutes, this can be quite exacting. As authors have become more numerous, more neurotic and less literate, so the editor's function in a publishing house has become specialized: some acquire blockbusters, some commission and others work on manuscripts whilst leaving the nannying to their underlings.

Each generation understands its own, sensing the mood, seeking out writers who express the feel of their times.

Tony Godwin was another classic 1960s whizzkid. He started a bookshop in the Charing Cross Road, which became the focus for the alternative society. He was picked up by Sir Allen Lane (q.v.), changed monochrome Penguin jackets into colour pix and was first to publish original fiction in paperback (it didn't work). He was inevitably, through the late Sir Allen Lane's jealousy of male talent, fired. He was hired by George Weidenfeld as chief editor, a seat equally hot as that position at André Deutsch, and ended bitterly in New York with a 'private' imprint at Harcourt, Brace, Jovanovich. Although he told me, a few weeks before he died, that he had only one friend in America ('an ethnic Lithuanian policeman in Rhodes [sic] Island'), he was a publisher so beloved that there is a transatlantic award in his name for promising young editors.

Today, Patrick Janson Smith at Corgi, Nick Webb, formerly at NEL, now running Arrow, Robert McCrum at Faber, Christopher Maclehose at Collins and Liz Calder at Cape, are all editors who will mould the taste of the future, selecting the manuscripts we will soon all be reading.

But one of the most striking editors around is Liz Calder: she has original taste and doesn't buy glitter. After starting as assistant story-editor for MGM, she went to Gollancz and then was called into Cape. It was she who first published Salman Rushdie (whose *Midnight's Children* was winner of the 1981 Booker Prize) with his largely ignored first novel, *Grimus*. Robyn Davidson, who trekked by camel across Australia from Alice Springs to Perth, is one of hers, as is Patrick Marnham, author of a classic travel book about Africa, *Fantastic Invasion*. Like many an English editor, she is building up her own list, although the situation here has not quite reached the level in America where publishing houses are so large that editors create their own 'private imprints' – like Elisabeth Sifton at Viking.

In New York the author/publisher relationship is less formal (McGraw-Hill is bigger than all the English trade publishers put together), editors are so significant that the author's agent sometimes insists on a contract with the publisher being dependent on the continued presence of the author's editor. If the editor is changed, the contract is void. This immeasurably increases the editor's power. There has been a reaction against this, against one editor getting too uppity, and committee publishing is the result whereby a board consisting of all the editors in the firm individually endorse each product before it is accepted for publication. Each editor thus has to sell his baby to the editorial committee. The whole editorial/author relationship in America is such that editors move from firm to firm taking 'their' authors with them, their wardrobe. Bob Gottlieb brought his whole wardrobe over to Knopf when he left Simon & Schuster.

In London, editors inspire less awe though quite as much affection. They too have been known to walk away with the authors on their list when moving to another house: they have also been known to move off and start their own imprint on the strength of the authors they have been building up with their old firm. For the bond joining a good editor and an author is powerful. Something of its strength can be gauged from Melvyn Bragg's long eulogy in *Punch* in praise of David Farrer of Secker & Warburg. Melvyn praised David for loving his authors' work, not uncritically, but kindly and honestly. David might ask an author to slice out twenty thousand words of his 'immortal and imperishable prose' but he did it with such charm and unfeigned affection that the author accepted his verdict.

'The reason why you trusted him,' wrote Melvyn Bragg, 'was that he saw the intention and sympathized: he read the execution and wanted to help . . . David would never sneer, nor be cleverer-than-thou, nor dismissive, nor be grand: he sought out what was good, rested his case on it and built on that.' An author is at his most vulnerable when he has just finished his manuscript –

> when it is out there on the start of a voyage which could lead to nowhere at all; when you have spilled out more than you wanted and yet done less than you had hoped; when you are wondering why the hell you did it and what on earth it *means*, then it was nice, very nice, when the phone went and the archly cultured voice would gently hawk out some of that day's poison before saying, 'I've just this moment finished it. And while I think there's work to be done – maybe quite a bit – I loved it! I especially enjoyed . . .'

Encouraging an author to produce the work he meant to write rather than the one he has written, is largely a psychological exercise requiring much tact and gentleness. Sometimes the manuscript that the author has produced is gargantuan, it would cost £25 a copy to print as it is; the author must be persuaded to see that he will make little impact at such a price for few will buy; with delicate care for his sensibilities he must be helped to cut, to condense, to précis and to discard.

Sometimes the intended book is too slim, a few cautious ideas casually jotted down. Fulco, Duke of Verdura, wished to write his memoirs of his childhood in Sicily, those idyllic years spent meandering in his grandmother's garden near Palermo, dressed in an Edwardian sailor suit from Peter Robinson, but after a few pages he was stuck. The editor went once a week to tea or to lunch to make suggestions: what did he do for Christmas, for his birthday, did he go abroad, did he keep any animals? One day, desperately trying to think of what a young Palermitan nobleman might have been up to at the beginning of the century, the editor threw out the name of the only Sicilian known to him, 'Did you ever come across Giuseppe de Lampedusa?' The reaction was instantaneous. 'Get out, get out! He was my second cousin and wrote THAT book about *my* great-grandparents. How dare you mention him . . . out, out!' Being an editor can be tricky.

Fay Weldon fears that 'the new young writer – that increasingly elusive creature – writes for the editor, not the readers . . . So the writer writes half-finished novels and says "What do you think, what shall I do?" And the editors say, because that is what they are employed to do: "Why, develop this character, or draw that one back, or change the end, or set it in Cardiff . . ."'

For the writer wishes to be heard and wants to reach as wide a public as possible. Equally the editor wants the book to be a success. Commercialism enters inevitably into both sides of the bargain. But the good editor knows that he must treat the delicate line between encouraging the author to be himself and urging him to be a little more saleable: the author is the creator, he must therefore, in a sense, be 'right', but the editor wants the book to be as near perfect as possible before it is put to the public and then he wants it to reach the widest possible audience. It is a very delicate two-way relationship which sadly often founders. The author sometimes feels he could manage without the infuriatingly bossy publisher, he would still continue to write and could, at a pinch, hand copies round as they do with Russian *samizdat* editions. (In Poland *samizdat* or underground publicity is highly organized and is favoured by authors not only for political reasons but because they are paid higher royalties.) In this country the publisher feels he is essential to the enterprise, longs to be loved but is ever conscious that he is grappling with too many titles, piracy, photocopying thieves, the rising price of paper and printing, fewer bookshops, library cuts and television, so he tends to be brusque and overbearing in order to get the author's book into the best commercial state possible. Love and praise are needed on both sides.

The need for an editor has arisen because of the decline too in the professionalism of the writer. Before the war, Hodder & Stoughton were alleged to send the latest John Buchan on to the printer unopened. Nowadays even such an accomplished trouper as Simon Raven, who has written nearly a book a year since 1958, needs and enjoys the attention of his editor.

Editing novels requires much more subtlety than working on non-fiction, for the novel is a work of creative imagination, the author's baby; to chop it about is like cutting off its arms and legs. Authors cannot imagine how their cherished offspring can possibly be wrong. Often, however, they themselves have laid the manuscript aside, coming back to it after a pause with quite different ideas in mind – which shows. Or they may have come to hate one of their characters and suddenly changed the whole balance of the book. Unable to invent an ending, the writer may just stop dead. Writer's block may be the problem: although this can be a euphemism for non-performance meaning that the writer is too bored, too lonely, too unloved to perform: hunger or flattery may be the cure.

Writers of non-fiction may spend several lonely years living with their subject until it becomes so much part of their thought process that they are unaware whether they have included some crucial point or not. Professors are capable of writing whole chapters round some issue whilst omitting the main point, so obvious is it to them. The editor must read carefully through the work of experts, checking for errors, for holes, for illogicality, for incomprehension, for muddled areas and *non sequiturs* before sitting down and persuading the author to make changes.

Careful editing is a slow process requiring supererogatory

patience and zeal. An editorial director will also have to attend committee meetings, think up new ideas, see to his old authors, read incoming books and race around enthusing about those in mid-gestation. He – increasingly she – will be hard pressed. If a vast tome now appears on his desk, commissioned perhaps five years previously, and needing a great deal of sorting out, he may well hand the work over to someone else: to a specialist who does nothing but editorial work and who is prepared to be at the beck and call of an author for three or four months' solid work. Finally, because of rising verbal inaccuracy from authors to compositors, preparation for press is left to that crucial and occasionally inspired drudge, the copy-editor.

These book surgeons are not to be confused with ghost writers: they do not write the books themselves but sit patiently beside the author, cajoling him into giving of his very best, persuading him that he can produce the masterpiece that is within him if he will only take more care. Dieter Pevsner, ex-Pelican, ex-Wildwood House, ex-Deutsch, has a most persuasive speech he used to make to professors and world experts whose magnum opera for Pelican were well-nigh incomprehensible in their erudition. He used to ask the specialist writer to imagine that his book had been bought by a Nobel prize-winner in physics who had as much, if not more intelligence than the author, but not his knowledge of the subject. The physicist could understand quickly but he needed to be led into the subject very gently, step by step. Perhaps he had bought the book to while away a long journey after a hard day's work, he was reading for pleasure so he wanted to enjoy himself; therefore the book must be clear and logical and recap at regular intervals, it must explain specialist vocabulary and sum up complex arguments, be lively and succinct. Dieter would then ask the writer to begin with these ideas in mind.

Busy editorial directors will not always have the time to read – let alone edit – everything that drops upon their desks. They will send out manuscripts to be read by others, usually people working at home who were once in the firm and whose judgment they trust. Jonathan Cape demand that all readers, whether part-time or full-time, work inside 32 Bedford Square. A good reader can make a publisher's list. Victor Gollancz has for years relied on the brilliant reports of Jon Evans. He reads from his home in Dorset nine or more books a week, and is as unfazeable today as he was when the old man hired him over fifty years ago. The Bodley Head have all manuscripts read in-house, but all readers wherever they sit, whatever else they do, must be known to the editorial director and understand precisely what he or she is looking for. The reader is after all trying to save editorial time, is reading *for* the editorial director, and so the reader's report must convey exactly the flavour of the manuscript, what kind of book it is, whether it is an outstanding, average or poor example of that kind, a résumé of the plot and – as there are so few original plots in the English language – how that plot has been approached. This information must be distilled swiftly and succinctly in a report which takes up as short a space as possible. Tony Godwin used to expect everything to be contained on one page. The report can comment on standard of writing, problems, howlers, errors, and any doubts it seems to raise, but if the reader is enthusiastic he must try to get across just why he wanted to turn each page. As the editor will have to write a letter about the book to whoever sent it in, it is useful if the reader has made some positive comment even if the report as a whole is negative.

Readers do not themselves accept or turn down: they give pointers, make suggestions, expose problems, signpost snags and try to reveal the nature of the product. Here is an example of a non-fiction report.

*Bob Dylan: Outside the Gates of Eden*

This is obviously an extremely good, detailed, insightful (sorry), and interesting book, covering all aspects of BD and his music. I found the analyses of the songs of his that I know (up to *Nashville Skyline*) very interesting and informative: the rest I have no knowledge of, but would expect the same quality.

The other reader puts the point that the symbolism

stuff, i.e. the parts where Watkins compares Rimbaud and Apollinaire to Dylan, is rather heavy and perhaps not suitable for ordinary Dylan fanatics. I suggest that this could all be rewritten together into an appendix or separate chapter as an 'extra'. The author would probably hate this, but these passages do hinder the flow of biography to comment to analysis that is so well done here. It is *extremely* well written.

As to market. There are a number of books on Dylan, of course. But I feel that this is so very good that it may compete very well. Is there any way of knowing what others have in the pipeline? This would also need an up-dated Epilogue.

What about Illustrations? An eight page in the middle would be nice, even just to show BD at the various stages written about in the book. One wouldn't really need much more than that. In this way it would fit into an ordinary format, also for paperback (perhaps large format paperback, for swish and price).

Would get very good reviews. Is the author good with publicity – this could be important for Peel-like chats . . .

Recommend further interest. (A problem with this title would be obtaining permission, crucial to understanding the text, to quote Dylan's heavily guarded lyrics.)

Clichés as you see are a useful means of conveying quickly what a book is like: Roget's *Thesaurus* is invaluable. The reader is not expected to have exceptional knowledge of any subject but is meant to assess for the general market and to know whether it is worth sending the book out for a specialist report. The publisher's reader is paid between £10 and £25 a book and is expected to return it within the week, whereas the professor or leading expert on a subject might get a fee of £100 or more. Busy pundits need persuading to get a move on, they are quite capable of keeping a manuscript gathering dust for months.

With fiction, the approach is slightly different. Here is an example of a fiction report:

*The Sweet Shop Owner* by Graham Swift (TS direct)

Unpromising title and subject matter, but a highly promising novel. Willy Chapman owns a newsagents in Sydenham; we follow him through his last day alive, at the end of which he deliberately overstrains his heart to bring on the fatal attack which has been threatening for so long. He sorts out his papers, pays off his delivery boys, spars with the beaky Mrs Cooper, his assistant, who has wanted to marry him for 16 years, reflects on the ephemeral nature of his trade – cigarettes, sweets, magazines, toys, all are disposable. Interspersed are memories of his difficult life: his marriage into a moneyed family; his relationship with his difficult wife, who is permanently ill but will not allow love into her scheme of things (it was she who bought him the shop); his tedious war service in the quartermaster's stores, counting tin helmets; the birth of their only daughter, and her growing up, beautiful but emotionally stunted in the loveless atmosphere; the eventual death of his wife and the battles with his daughter over the will. The passage of time is beautifully conveyed by the minutiae of his life – the price of cigarettes, the changing character of the shopping street around him, the clothes of the children who come in to buy sweets, the headlines in the papers he sells but never reads – these last also serve as an ironic counterpoint to his own life: PEACE BID FAILS reads one at a particularly difficult stage.

This strikes me as an exceptional first novel – beautifully written, intelligent, extraordinary in the way it creates something out of nothing. I found myself really caring about this South London newsagent and his commonplace life, which is no small achievement. I think Mr Swift is someone with a future.

Recommended.

Even such a glowing report did not persuade the publishers to accept this unsolicited manuscript, but now Mr Swift nestles with Heinemann and has been a Booker Prize runner-up.

The outside reader does not know anything about the money involved, who has offered the book, nor any other details, so he or she is not in a position to make assertive statements. Occasionally a book comes with a directive asking for certain points to be looked at very carefully with the implication that opinions are divided inside the publishing house. Then the reader is not asked to give the story, merely to comment, to help others make up their minds: to be the devil's advocate.

Melvyn Bragg wrote that the work of a writer 'is solitary, it can be full of pleasure but equally it can be full of stress. It is, by definition, lonely. They are, by definition, utterly dependent on themselves. No one will finish the book for them. In most cases no one is especially waiting for the book. Unwritten, the book will make no ripple of loss. When it is done it is not necessarily over. When it is delivered it is far from finished. When it is published it might be a beginning or an end.' They need their editors to bring them help and comfort and praise, they need readers and book surgeons who will be positive and useful but above all they would like recognition and a good, clean, straightforward contract with a publisher.

# VI *Contracts*

The manuscript has been written, a literary agent has been found who likes it and he or she has now submitted it to a publisher. Or the author may have sent his work directly to a publisher of his choice. The publisher has read the manuscript, or had it read, has expressed initial enthusiasm and has made suitably encouraging noises. With luck, the publisher will now write a letter accepting the manuscript for publication and offering the author a legal contract. This will either be done directly, or indirectly through the author's literary agent. The publisher may not print the book for public sale until he has leased the copyright of the book from the author for reproduction. The author holds inalienable copyright in his or her creation; this is registered in the book when it is published by the simple sign © next to the author's name in the preliminary pages, as can be seen on page iv of this book. Even if the creation is only a letter, the copyright still belongs to whoever wrote it. The letter may be written and sent by A to B and then sold years later by Sotheby's, but it still may not be reproduced without A's permission.

This copyright is infinitely divisible and like a freehold can be sub-let in return for a fee or royalty. The royalty is based on the retail published price of the book and usually begins at 10 per cent. In return for this 10 per cent, the author licenses a publisher to sell his books in certain qualified markets – only in the Isle of Wight if he so wishes. (Rosemary

Buckman, the multilingual publisher's agent operating from a cottage in Oxfordshire, sold the Lithuanian language rights of a book with the territory restricted to the USA.) If the publisher prices a book at £10, then the author should get £1 a copy. If, however, the author has an agent, that agent will first deduct 10 per cent for himself before passing the money on, so the author will in fact only be getting 90p a copy. The net of the £10 after booksellers' discount goes to the publisher to cover paper, printing, binding, book jacket, publishing overheads, advertising, distributing and selling to the wholesalers, retailers, libraries and bookshops, and profit. If the publisher has given the author an advance payment of £1,000, the author will not start getting any royalty money until this advance has been earned, that is, until 1,000 copies have been sold.

Royalties are paid on copyrights for fifty years after the author's death to whomsoever the author has designated to receive them in his will. It may be a member of the family, an executor, a lover. In the case of *Peter Pan*, now being filmed by Steven Spielberg, J. M. Barrie designated Great Ormond Street Hospital for Sick Children, and in the case of *Winnie the Pooh*, A. A. Milne left his royalties after his death to the Garrick Club. These benign, and, to some, essential institutions may get quite a shock when the money dries up.

Fay Weldon professes to find it extraordinary that her creative work, published perhaps when she was twenty, should still be making money for her publisher and literary agent when she is ninety or even under the sod and so not able to enjoy a penny herself. She suggests that a ten-year lease would be more sensible. Television companies can take two-year leases. Piers Paul Read feels that the benefit of copyright, like every other form of property, should continue in perpetuity. It is not always understood that the writer's share is based on a sum of money – the cover price of the book – which the publisher never sees. Out of his share, the publisher has to give bookshops, retailers, wholesalers and overseas customers an average discount of 42 per cent; some paperback wholesalers insist on discounts of 62½ per cent.

It is possible to sell the foreign rights in a bestseller to twenty, thirty or forty different countries. At the New Delhi book fair, I once sold the rights to translate *Small is Beautiful* by E. F. Schumacher into Bengali, Gujerati and Kerala. I may have only made a dent in India's fourteen main languages but the advance was £50 a throw, which soon tots up.

Not all countries in the world have signed the international copyright laws. Copyright is currently menaced to the tune of £500 million a year, the Publishers Association estimate, from piracy, which is particularly virulent in the Far East, especially Taiwan. The Nigerians, the Chinese, and schools and universities using photocopying machines are the latest culprits.

An interesting twist to the problem of protecting copyright from being ripped off by institutions is to sell the right to reproduce with the book and adjust the price upwards accordingly. So Jonquil Publishing have produced a 28 pp *Guide to Money Management* for sale at £8.50!

Voyaging on the SS *Ben Cruachan* from Nagoya to Colombo, I was examining a copy of the marine engineer's *vade mecum* and thought some cigarette ash had fallen on the page. I made to flick it off but it would not move. It must have fallen off the cigarette of the pirate in Singapore who had been photographing this vast, expensive and crucial tome. No doubt he had then sold it to young officers for a quarter of the Edinburgh publisher's original price. Publishers, like video producers, rant against this infringement of copyright. Perhaps they could learn from the Performing Rights Society, which polices the royalties of composers and lyricists far more efficiently and ruthlessly than any publisher.

Before the Soviet Union signed the 1973 copyrights agreement roubles had to be collected in person and occasionally were, leading to splendid binges. One cannot wait for China, some of whose 1,000 million might like our books in translation, to follow suit.

Authors wishing to quote from one another must observe 'fair dealing', a rule of thumb whereby a total of 800 words (of which no more than 300 are consecutive) or an extract not exceeding 400 words may be quoted without obtaining permission provided the source is credited. Permission is usually given for longer extracts if due acknowledgment is made, sometimes for a fee. It is usual, though, to ask permission of the copyright holder when making many quotations, otherwise it may look like plagiarism, which is stealing from the works of another. At most a quarter of a poem (or 40 lines if that is less) may be quoted before obtaining permission; again, acknowledgment is required. Poets usually charge a fee if the whole of one of their poems is quoted, particularly if it is used in an anthology. Why not, it is an important source of income for them. I would like to have quoted, in this book, Fay Weldon's whole speech which she made at the Booker prizegiving and which appeared in *The Times*, but her agent wanted £20–£25 per thousand words for Commonwealth rights, £30–£35 per thousand words for USA rights and £50–£60 per thousand words for world rights. It is perfectly permissible to quote short passages in reviews and critical articles without paying or asking permission. This is not the case with television, where rival companies are not encouraged to film excerpts belonging to each other, even for reviewing purposes; which is why there are no good critical television review programmes.

The average solicitor is baffled by a publisher's contract, which can have anything from fifteen to fifty clauses. However, in day-to-day business the only significant parts are those concerned with the advance, the royalty rate and the division of subsidiary rights. Those outside the business are apt to get jumpy about the libel clause, penalties for late delivery of the manuscript by the author if it is a commissioned book, and the standard option clause which asks the author to offer the publisher his next similar work, but these are of less importance. Here are some specific points.

The publisher's advance payment is *against*, not on top of, royalties; a point frequently misunderstood. It is a sum of money paid ahead of time to the author in anticipation that the royalties on the cover price will be earned. For instance a publisher may pay £1,000 to an author on delivery of a synopsis (or, in American jargon, a proposal) which it is hoped will form the basis of a book to be published when it is written in six or nine months' time. This sum of money is generally irrecoverable by the publisher should the book never materialize: it is a punter's risk. There are, in the little world that publishers inhabit, 'advance-takers': attractive, winsome folk who come up with glamorous ideas but have no serious intention of delivering the painfully laborious back-up words. The success of the confidence trickster depends on the greed and optimism of the victims. Publishers are lulled by the sound of *Zukunft Musik*. They want an early note to develop into a symphony. They are often wrong. The cost of being polite to dim authors and of being conned by sharp ones is never reckoned by authors' organizations. That is the publisher's risk. When you consider that many publishers commission over one-third of their non-fiction list each year, then you begin to see that publishers are not the staid old misers many people seem to think.

The royalty rate on an average novel is calculated on the cover price of the book and might be 10 per cent on the published price of the first 2,500 copies sold to the general public within the British Isles, 12½ per cent on the next 2,500 copies sold and 15 per cent on all subsequent copies sold. On copies going abroad for export, the royalty might be a flat rate throughout of 10 per cent of the price received, if bought in quantity by an overseas publisher.

If it is a first novel and sells very few copies, it might not even earn the money which the kind publisher advanced to the author when he delivered his manuscript. Many books never do earn even their advances. Once, however, this advance has been paid off, publishers should send cheques and statements to their authors at six-monthly intervals. People often wonder how trustworthy the publisher's statements of copies sold are, since all evidence for their compilation is in the hands of those writing out the cheques, but publishers are not usually suspected of cooking the books. Many years ago the late Paul Elek's imprint hit a very bad patch, royalties ceased to flow. However, business eventually picked up and an efficient and honourable accountant made sure that authors did indeed eventually get their money – late but unbouncing.

Publishers accept that they may well only break even on

the volume sales of their books: their profit comes from the sales of subsidiary rights, which can be anything from a film deal running to hundreds of thousands of dollars to giving permission for a book to be sold to the partially sighted in LARGE PRINT for £600. (No charge is made for braille editions.) Publishers take a variety of percentages on subsidiary rights: routinely they try for 50 per cent of the paperback rights, but, increasingly on big books, can be whittled down to 25 per cent; 10 per cent of film rights or 10 per cent of first serial rights if the book is to be run in cut form in one of the Sunday newspapers or in a magazine for the first time; 50 per cent for anthology rights is generally accepted.

Subsidiary rights clauses may vary but the clause granting the publisher total control over the book's jacket-design seldom does. It is no use the author insisting that his niece, who was short-listed for Camberwell Art School, should paint a picture for the jacket; the publisher will decide. He may not be the printer, nor the bookseller, but he is the impresario. Diaghilev told Nijinsky, Stravinsky and Picasso what to do, he even insisted on exploring the personalities of his prettier ballerinas in depth – so Lord Weidenfeld will decide what goes on Lord Olivier's dust jacket. The publisher also, incidentally, decides what will go on the jacket's inside front flap, the blurb. Occasionally the author may be asked to draft an initial version, but he has no *rights* to a say in the final form.

There is a clause in every author's contract which asks him to guarantee that nothing in his book is libellous. The English libel laws are the envy of the litigious throughout the world. Milton Obote, once Ugandan leader, won £40,000 in damages because he was mentioned libellously in a book about Amin. Sir James Goldsmith has received, not that he needs it, tens of thousands of pounds from *Private Eye* between 1977 and 1983. Richard Ingrams, the editor of *Private Eye*, swims upstream in a river of libel like an experienced trout and has become a great authority on the subject.

Libel can occur if what is written about a person brings him or her into hatred, ridicule or contempt and shows malice or causes financial damage. An ideal libel action would be if a rival published a neat joke about a medical colleague, identifying everyone and saying, 'If the patient can keep awake Mr Anaesthetist, so can you,' naming names, giving date and place. Publishers are understandably nervous of libel since the law is both woolly and expensive. With Leon Brittan as Home Secretary it might be thought that there is a chance of reform since he is a QC, expert in libel, a civilized fellow and, like the President of Israel, a former Guards officer. Sadly he may have better (or worse) things to do.

Piers Paul Read invented a character for his novel *Polonaise* called Lord Derwent, who wasn't put over as being very attractive. Read lives in North Yorkshire, so does Lord Derwent, at Hackness Hall, Scarborough, to be precise. Oh dear.

Many years ago a book called *Greek Tragedy* by A. Heckstall Smith described how three brigadiers flew to Cairo from Piraeus leaving their brigades behind them. To be fair to these distinguished soldiers, when the book came out they only asked the publishers to apologize in the High Courts. Nevertheless, a director of the publishing house, with his solicitor in tow, visited their General Officer Commanding, Field-Marshal Lord ('Jumbo') Wilson of Libya, to ask him if he recalled the incident. 'Yes,' replied that much-loved and very splendid Englishman.

'I should have had 'em shot.'

The publisher's eyes gleamed. 'Will you say that, Sir, in a court of law?'

'Yes,' said the Field-Marshal.

'Ah, but,' muttered the solicitor when out in the street later, 'the cost of apologizing in the High Courts is around £50, but to defend an action successfully could run you to over £2,500.'

The costs of litigation in English courts of law are so high that it doesn't pay to be in the right, even if you can prove it. The publisher therefore took the easy and cowardly way out.

I know because I was the publisher and this story can only be told because the brigadiers are safely in their graves.

Here is a case which is unique in legal history. In 1973 we published a paperback for 50p, which was ghosted (brilliantly in three weeks by David Wynne-Morgan); it was the autobiography of the most famous tart, an Irish girl, who politically ruined that top and most eloquent of aristos, Tony Lambton, who could have been the Earl of Durham. (For further details on him see *Who's Really Who* edited by Richard Compton, published by Frederick Muller, Blond & Briggs, 1983.)

If Lord Lambton was Norma's most distinguished private client, then the names of her internationally-known customers read like the guest list for some State funeral, for she was, if not the government whore, employed indirectly by the Foreign Office to service visiting Heads of State.

> One evening when President Soekarno was on an official visit to London with a delegation of high-ranking Indonesians, I was one of three girls who were booked to go and have dinner with him in a suite at Grosvenor House. I was sent for Soekarno himself because he had particularly asked for a tall, slim girl. That was unusual as we found that the Indonesians normally wanted girls who were short and slightly on the plump side.

Alas, Norma, whose recollections, when checked as they had to be in this contentious and doomed publication, turned out to be amazingly accurate, had got one thing wrong. It was not an official visit and so his widow (sixth wife and former Tokyo prostitute) was able to maintain that the President had not been in London in the relevant period. That apology cost £500 (inflation). A week later our manuscript editor Sheila Thompson, now a high flier at the Ministry of Defence, was telling the tale to an Indonesian friend who owned a shop in Bond Street specializing in Orientalia. 'What a pity,' she was told, 'he was in here only the other day.' Nevertheless, as a general rule, cowardice is cheaper.

Clauses requiring the author to return an advance are rarely invoked (except by André Deutsch*), ditto penalties for late delivery by the author and delayed publication by the pub-

* At the time of writing the author and Mr Deutsch are in litigation on this particular subject, so some allowance must be made for personal animus.

lisher. Until recently the standard option clause in contracts was equally unenforceable, being usually not much more than an agreement to agree that the publisher be offered the author's next work on a similar subject. Indeed, until the André Brink case there had been no case history at all on the subject. The André Brink affair is so special and illustrative of the way the publishing game is played that each move in it should be recorded.

On a trip to South Africa, Mr Donald Morrison, Sales Director of W. H. Allen, was recommended by a South African bookseller to look at a novel by an Afrikaans university don called André Brink. He showed it to his Managing Director, Jeffrey Simmons, in England, who enthusiastically published it under the title *Looking on Darkness*. It won, as they say, literary acclaim and correspondingly modest sales, but Jeffrey Simmons personally sold American rights to William Morrow & Co. in New York. W. H. Allen had recently been bought by an American entrepreneur and a *lawyer* known as 'Smiley' Ralph Fields. Fields redrafted W. H. Allen's publishing contracts and introduced into the option clause – after the routine preamble which describes the author, known in publishing contracts, for reasons explained above, as 'the Proprietor' – the following crucial words:

> provided that the Proprietor shall not subsequently accept from any other publisher terms less favourable than those offered by the Publisher, and provided that the Proprietor shall notify the Publisher of its proposed acceptance of any other publisher's terms and offer to the Publisher in priority to such other publisher upon the terms negotiated with such other publisher the right to publish the work and to have the other rights comprised in this Agreement over such work such offer to remain open for a period of one month.

Aubrey Davies, an editor, left W. H. Allen not long after Jeffrey Simmons himself departed and joined the literary agency of Hughes Massie, taking André Brink with him as a client. Brink's next novel was so good that Mr Davies decided to have an auction (q.v.). He did not allow W. H. Allen to take part in the event (one must suppose they had had some sort of tiff) and young master Robert McCrum of Faber & Faber was the successful bidder. For the first time in history the original publisher, Ralph Fields, sued and was paid £30,000 in an out-of-court settlement. Phew! Watch the small print.

The Society of Authors, handlers of the estate of Bernard Shaw, stately, old and established, and the Writers' Guild, bedrabbled (Michael Holroyd), and waggish (Brigid Brophy), combined to produce a dream contract which they hoped would become the basis for argument between authors and their publishers, publishers and their authors, depending on whose side one is on. The BBC have accepted a modified version of this charter of authors' rights for the hundred or so publications they issue each year, so also have Faber & Faber. (Hamish Hamilton and W. H. Allen had both signed earlier versions of the Writers' Guild contract before it combined with the Society of Authors.)

Here are some of the more contentious clauses contained in the original draft which was sent to publishers for discussion, together with my own contentious and rather boring comments offered as those of a small publisher who wishes to stay in business. All but the most fiendish contract buffs should advance directly to Chapter VII. (Permission to print extracts from the *Minimum Terms Book Agreement* has been given.)

Incidentally this agreement has no agency clause – do they wish to dish agents, for they do not refer to them? Or do they imagine that authors will dispense with agents once they have received these terms from their publishers?

Clause A states that

> This agreement contains the minimum terms and conditions to be observed in all contracts between publishers and all members of the Society of Authors and all members of the Writers' Guild in respect of any original literary work published in hardcover volume form but excluding the following categories:
>
> 1. Illustrated books defined as books which would not have been published save for the illustrations.

2. Technical books, manuals, reference works.
3. Textbooks written for the educational market.
4. Books involving three or more writers.
5. Plays and poetry.

Big illustrated non-books and coffee-table supports do not normally allow for royalty agreements anyway; the writers may be on the payroll or given an outright fee and the same usually applies to those in section 2. Those mentioned in 3, whom the Americans call schoolbook authors, are in a separate – often much richer – category from general authors and have a much lower royalty scale and a much larger and more often repeated print run. Poets too have their own lore and laws.

> Clause B: The terms and conditions of the contract shall be no less favourable to the Author nor in any way detract from or qualify the terms and conditions specified in Section C hereof.

Surely a contract is a contract is a contract? The concept here is very Japanese.

> Clause C 1 (a): The Author shall deliver a script which, in style and content, is professionally competent and fit for publication.

But who will decide whether or not the manuscript is fit for publication? If not the publisher, he is emasculated.

> Clause C 1 (b): The Publishers shall notify the Author of any changes required in the script within thirty days. Should the Publishers reject the script on the ground that it fails to meet the specifications in (a) above, they shall within thirty days provide the Author with written notice of not less than 250 words in which grounds for rejecting the script shall be set out in such a manner as to facilitate arbitration.

This is fine, but authors and publishers are slapdash over the nitty-gritty and where are the penalties?

> Clause C 1 (d): Should the Author fail to meet the delivery date specified, the Publishers may give the Author six months' notice in writing to deliver the work and should he fail to do so the Publishers shall be entitled to terminate the contract in which event any advance shall be returnable and all rights shall revert to the Author.

The prospect of authors returning advances they have inevitably spent is dim.

> Clause C 2: The Author shall indemnify the Publishers against any loss, injury or damage resulting from any breach by the Author (unknown to the Publishers) of the warranty, provided that any legal costs and expenses and any compensation, damages, costs and disbursements shall be paid by the Publishers only on the joint advice of the respective legal advisers of the Author and the Publishers and failing agreement on the advice of Counsel selected and instructed jointly on behalf of the Publishers and the Author. The extent of the Author's indemnity shall not exceed the total monies received by the Author under the contract.

Supposing the author has (unconsciously) plagiarized. Why should his indemnity be limited?

> Clause 3 (a): The Publishers shall pay any copyright fees for illustrations and/or quotations up to maximum of £x, any further sum being paid by the Publishers but deducted from the Author's royalties.

Copyright fees for photographs can be costly. If the successful book depends to an extent on its illustrations, the publisher must be sure that the expense is shared.

> Clause 4: The copyright in the work shall remain the property of the Author who shall grant to the Publishers

> the sole and exclusive right for a period of ten years from the date of the contract or delivery of the script (whichever is the later) to print, publish and sell the work in volume form.

Why should the sub-licences be limited to ten years? If the book is any good, they should be allowed to run for the full fifty-year term. This, like many other clauses, will, if accepted, lead to a mountain of filing cabinets. If the book doesn't sell, the copyright is worthless anyway.

> Clause 5: The Publishers shall publish the work at their own expense and risk, in a first edition consisting of the number of copies named in approximate terms in the contract within twelve months.

No publisher who wishes to stay solvent should sign this clause. There is many a lengthy slip twixt the signing of the contract and publication. Three weeks may be a long time in politics but twelve months can be the twinkling of an eye in publishing.

> Clause 6 (b): The Publishers shall obtain the Author's approval of copy editing, blurb, catalogue copy, number and type of illustrations, jacket design and publication date, such approval not to be unreasonably withheld or delayed.

Unacceptable. It is polite to consult, but, in the event of a dispute, a publisher must be in control of this area totally. You do not ask parents to be the judges of a baby contest.

> Clause 8: The Publishers shall use their best endeavours to market the work effectively . . . and shall do everything they reasonably can to ensure that copies are ready for sale in all leading bookshops by publication day.

Teaching your grandmother to suck eggs. If the publisher hasn't managed this, there is nothing the author can do about it.

> Clause 10 (a): The Publishers shall pay the Author an advance against royalties which shall be calculated as follows:
>
> (i) On account of the Publishers' own editions: not less than 65% of the Author's estimated receipts from the sale of the projected first printing.

This I find reasonable, oddly enough. Publishers often knowingly pay in advance more than the book could earn on the first print, provided, of course, they have a fair share of the subsidiary rights.

> Clause 10 (b): In the case of a commissioned work half the advance shall be paid on signature of the contract and half within one year of signature or on publication, whichever is the sooner.

This is a hopeless attempt to standardize an immense variety of situations. Some authors are non-deliverers and the only incentive to perform is the lure of lucre. By paying half the money down, the publisher halves his carrot and his stick.

> Clause 13 (b): Should the Publishers sub-license paperback rights to an independent paperback publisher, all monies accruing under such sub-licence shall be divided in the proportion 60% to Author, 40% to Publishers on the first £5,000 accruing under the sub-licence, and 70% to the Author and 30% to the Publishers thereafter.

The proportion of paperback royalties between author and publisher is an ancient battle. It has always been the publisher's line that fifty-fifty was the only possible ratio. There was a complex gentlemen's agreement that this should not be infracted. I broke it over *The Carpetbaggers* when I agreed to accept two guineas a thousand on the grounds that where the hardback publisher was not at risk, he could reduce his share of a bestselling paperback. The same thinking surely still applies and if a publisher is taking on a first novel, he should surely be granted a generous share of the gravy, if any.

Indeed, the whole subsidiary rights income should be set against the advance.

> Clause 15 (a): If the Author grants to the Publishers US rights in the work, they shall make every effort to arrange the publication of an American edition of the work on a royalty basis. The Publishers shall retain not more than 15% of the proceeds from any such edition inclusive of any sub-agent's commission. Should the Publishers fail to negotiate publication of an American edition on a royalty basis, but obtain an offer for an edition at a price inclusive of the Author's remuneration, they shall pay the Author not less than 12½% of their net receipts.

If the above applies in 13 (b) then 15 per cent is simply not enough. Indeed there is no reason why there can't be a happy publishing relationship based on Brian Epstein's '50 per cent and friendship' with the Beatles.

> Clause 17 (a): If the Author grants to the Publishers an exclusive licence to handle the following rights on his behalf the Publishers shall pay to the Author the following percentages of the proceeds:

| | | |
|---|---|---|
| (i) | Second, i.e. post volume publication serial rights | 80% |
| (ii) | Anthology and quotation rights | 60% |
| (iii) | Condensation rights | 75% |
| (iv) | Strip cartoon rights | 75% |

That the publisher has no share of the first serial rights, the most lucrative, is monstrous. There would be no first serial rights in the book, if there was not a book.

> Clause 19 (d): The Publishers shall make no deduction from monies due to the Author other than those provided for herein. In the event of late payment, the Publishers shall pay interest on the monies overdue at the rate of 3% above the base rate of the major clearing banks.

Clause 19 (e): The Author or his authorised representative shall have the right upon written request to examine the Publishers' books of account in so far as they relate to the work, which examination shall be at the cost of the Author unless errors exceeding 2% of the total sums paid to the Author shall be found to his disadvantage in which case the costs shall be paid by the Publishers.

Many clauses like these are recipes for ill-will. Incidentally, computers are so expensive to program, that many American publishers pay royalties on the difference between their inventory and their print number, including free copies.

Clause 22: The Publishers shall not assign the rights granted to them in the contract or the benefit thereof without the Author's written consent.

A red light should glow here for the nervous and prudent publisher. Not being able to assign his copyrights without renovation could impede a merger and make a bankruptcy more horrible.

Clause 25: Any dispute arising in connection with the contract shall be referred to a joint committee composed of a representative of the Society of Authors, a representative of the Writers' Guild and two representatives appointed by the Publishers but not connected with their company, whose unanimous decision shall be binding. Failing unanimous agreement, the dispute shall be referred to a single arbitrator appointed by the above named parties and the decision of the arbitrator shall be binding. Failing agreement on the choice of a single arbitrator, the dispute shall be referred to the London Court of Arbitration under its rules.

God help us all.

Clause 26: The Author shall not grant the Publishers an option or first refusal on any of his future works.

Option clauses are toothless anyway except that devised by Mr Ralph Fields of W. H. Allen. It is just that the tone of voice here sounds unfriendly. As cannot be said too often, a publisher's contract is but an agreement of two friendly, nay doting and dependent, parties to agree.

To sum up: this dream contract suggests royalties of at least 10 per cent of the bookshop price; advance payments amounting to more than half the book's expected income (this would mean more than £5,000 for a £10 book of which 10,000 copies were printed); and the lion's share of earnings from all paperback and foreign editions. It also suggests that the publisher cannot reject a manuscript if it conforms with the terms of the contract and that he must publish within twelve months of receiving it or compensate the author. Publishers must now pay towards the cost of indexing and illustrations and consult the author on editing, design and display.

It will be interesting to see which publishers follow the example of the BBC and Faber & Faber.

# VII *Five facets of publishing*

Five recent phenomena in publishing are packaging, the trade paperback, computer publishing, the auction and book clubs. Here we go.

## *Packaging*

Publishers which have huge overheads, their own sales force their own warehouses, welcome a ready-made product tha they can slot into their machine which is hungry for turnover Hence the packager. Recent successes are *The Country Diary of an Edwardian Lady* and the illustrated *Lark Rise to Candle-ford*. The packaged book is always highly illustrated, heavily edited and, since the packager has access to the top freelance talent, it often looks better than the in-house product. (A further extension of the packaging idea is merchandizing, when the illustrations used by the packager are sold to others to put on china, clothing or whatever. For more details on this, see Chapter X.)

Oxford University Press originally published the hardback edition of *Lark Rise to Candleford* in 1939; it has not only sold over a quarter of a million copies in paperback but ha been made into a play by the National Theatre Company and will no doubt soon appear on the box. OUP sold the abridged illustrated rights only to Anthony Cheetham of Century who n turn asked the packaging house of Shuckburgh Reynolds .o turn it into a Victorian period presentation, awash with ɔld photographs, paintings and pressed flowers. (They in turn ɩave persuaded Debenhams to launch harmonious merchan-lise such as cottage furniture, smocks, herbal cosmetics, jams ınd cakes to tie in with Flora Thompson's descriptions.)

That is an example of an already well known and admired itle being enhanced still further by extra illustration in order o sell additional copies, taking advantage of the current :nthusiasm for nostalgia and romantic country imagery. Iowever, it is possible to make up the package first and then ;ell the whole idea to the publisher. To find out how this vorked, I went along to see Robert MacDonald, who lives ıt the top of a twisted iron staircase in the bowels of a Knightsbridge mews. He pays twenty pounds a week rent and ıis IBM typewriter is a 'legacy' from Collins, his former :mployer. He left that house because the routine of list-filling, lepartmentalization and lack of scope bored him, 'the best ›art of the day was lunchtime'.

He says that, logically, the enormous cost of an editorial lepartment should mean that mainline publishers will become listributors of one-off projects, in the same way that Channel 4 funds programmes from independent producers.

It is to be hoped, by those who favour the survival of the ›ook as an object of art if not quality, that this dictum does ıot become absolute, because the average product concocted ›y the packager is a highly illustrated book of topical appeal vith a likely TV link – not something which will linger in the ace of eternity.

'A packager', says MacDonald, 'has only, needs only, his vits to live on.' Dorling Kindersley, one of the twenty-three nentioned in *Writers' and Artists'*, conceived the archetypal ›ackaged book – *The Amateur Naturalist* by Gerald Durrell. A popular subject by a popular writer. The Formula goes like his: nobble your famous author on a favourite subject (the vriting should not be too much of a strain); tempt with :nough of a tit-bit, with a promise of more money upfront hould the project get off the ground, ditto with a designer ınd a researcher. Coax a printer into producing a dummy, shop it around complete with jacket to publishers in London New York and at Frankfurt and simultaneously try and fix up a book club who may prod a publisher (this is a new twist to the tail wagging the dog). This, plus the reassurance of a joint bank account, and a convinced printer, should persuade a publisher to commit himself to an outlay, on the whole greater than he would dare on an internal project, and the packager is on his way. In the case of *The Amateur Naturalist* Hamish Hamilton advanced £40,000. The book was a success, selling 170,000 copies at £12.50. The packager had succeeded in selling a book which everybody had thought of but nobody had actually done. His or her time is costed on a personal (i.e. low) and not on a company (i.e. high) rate. The packager should be left with some cosy residual rights round the clock and can, unlike an employed editor, swan off to the South China Seas to think of another scheme in peace.

The development of the packager, generally a small if not a one-man outfit, must be seen alongside the growth of the dining-room publisher. The business is polarized. It coalesce and merges at one end, fragments at the other.

Perhaps some idea of a packager's costings should be given to explain the level of sales needed if there is going to be a reasonable return. Take a hardback selling at £8.95, a trade edition of 25,000. Then the publisher's approximate buying in cost from the packager would be £2.56, which would be made up of 50p for royalties (£12,500); 0.515p for profit plus overheads at 25 per cent (£2,875); manufacturing at £ and plant at 0.545p (£13,625). These calculations have been based on the assumption that the author is paid on a royalty basis rather than an outright fee, which is not always necessarily the case, and that the publisher's mark-up is a factor of 3.5. Manufacturing costs would be cheaper if done in the Far East but are here based on a maximum of 160 pages, sewn jacketed, with full colour throughout.

The total figure of £13,625 for plant is not an assessment of how much the book would cost to put together, it is what is left when everything else is allocated – so provides working budget which determines what can and cannot b afforded. No allowance has been made for book club or US sales.

Alternatively, take a limpback selling at £5.95 in an edition of 50,000 – again, trade only. Here the publisher's buying-in cost would be £1.70 broken down to a royalty of 0.25p (£12,500), profit plus overhead at 0.29p (£14,500); manufacturing 0.80p and plant 0.36p. N.B. A (likely) book club sale alters these figures.

If you compare the costs for the publisher between an inside job and one bought in from the packager, you will now readily see why packaging occurs. Publishers' overheads obviously vary a bit, but 45 per cent for a full overhead allocation and 30 per cent for a sales overhead is probably about average in this day and age for any large general trade house, whereas plant costs are assumed to be the same for publisher and packager:

| | *inside* | *bought in* |
|---|---|---|
| Retail price | 8·95 | 8·95 |
| Net receipts @ 40% discount | 5·37 | 5·37 |
| Royalty @ 10% | ·895 | none |
| Overheads @ 45% and 30% resp. | 2·42 | 1·61 |
| Plant | ·545 | none |
| Publicity | ·20 | ·20 |
| Manufacturing | 1·00 | 2·56 |
| TOTAL COST | 5·06 | 4·37 |
| PROFIT | ·31 | 1·00 |
| | (5·8%) | (18·6%) |

## *The trade paperback*

Hardbacks are fast becoming antiques affordable only by the middle-aged, librarians and schools. Is any binding worth more than 100 per cent on the price? However, hardbacks are expensive not just because they have stiff board covers, their print run is smaller. They are considered to contain new ideas, which means that they get reviewed and hence the public are made aware of their existence. Paperbacks are rapidly taking over because they are cheap, mass produced, printed in large numbers, sold in quantity, thanks often to the publicity engendered by their hardcover predecessors, and available in airport lounges, newsagents, Woolworths and on station bookstalls. Now a hybrid has appeared, the upmarket trade paperback, often only mildly floppy with an elegant old master on the front. Some are produced by hardback houses like Hodder & Stoughton, Collins, Routledge & Kegan Paul (who are calling their new imprint Ark); others are brought out by the paperback publishers under separate imprints: Sphere call theirs Abacus, Pan's is Picador. Virago's successful issue of originals and re-issue of classics has been matched by other imprints, notably Century with their travel books.

We live in a visually conscious age; television has made us hyper-aware of the 'image'. Many of these hybrid trade paperbacks are illustrated and thus are expected to appeal to sections of both the old hardback and the old mass markets: the print run is larger than that for a stiff cover, whilst the price is cheaper. Many are originals, others are brought out simultaneously with a hardback edition to scoop up the wider market.

The idea behind the trade paperback is to enable the publisher to be more flexible and to gain additional revenue for authors. Literary editors have been slow to give editorial space to reviews of original books which come out in this format.

The break between the mass-market paperback and the trade paperback is so marked in America that an upmarket trade paperback house will try to sell its mass-market rights to another house. For instance, Howard Kaminsky, ex-Lake Tahoe croupier, the most vibrant publisher in Manhattan, who ran Warner Books, has for many years tried to buy the mass paperback rights to *Small is Beautiful* from Torch, owned by Harper & Row, but they won't sell. This style of behaviour has yet to reach England.

Penguins have of course been in the trade paperback game for years. They are now part of Lord Cowdray's Pearson group, which includes Longmans in England and Viking

Penguin in New York. The bird family extends to Puffins, Peregrines, Kestrels and Pelicans. Dieter Pevsner, son of the famous German country-house plodder, as former editor of Pelican, attributed their success to the guilty conscience of the affluent. A traveller on the 07.55 Pullman to Manchester buys a Pelican on *Inner City Decay*, reads two pages, then relaxes with *Playboy*. As proof of this I have pristine pre-war Pelicans, still in their jackets and unopened. The whole Penguin aviary is now run by the American Peter Mayer, who jazzed up the place with much additional plumage: with the highest salary in publishing plus a percentage (which everyone acknowledges he deserves), he is a very grand keeper indeed.

Birds seem popular names: after Fontana Collins created Flamingo. Originally designed to put out their own books in paper, Fontana now competes in the general market and has a particularly good line in history. After Collins purchased Sidney Bernstein's Granada imprint, Fontana and Flamingo gained many new half-brothers including Dragon, Mayflower, Paladin and Panther – a polyglot menagerie.

Coronet is owned by Hodder & Stoughton, which has reinforced its market thrust by taking over the NEL from the New American Library, once owned by the Times-Mirror group, the biggest media operators in the world, Bertelsmann of Germany being number two with Corgi (Transworld) and Bantam of New York (once owned by Fiat) and Storychair and Carousel. Silhouette romances – quite hot for them – have been bought from Simon & Schuster by the wise birds at Mills & Boon.

Pan is jointly owned by Macmillan, Collins and Heinemann, with a third each. They have Piccolo for children, Picador for upmarket titles and Pavanne for Cosmo women.

Now everybody's doing it, often hard and soft together.

## Computer books

The government has encouraged schools, by means of grants, to own micro-computers and many already have computers for which they now need software. Longmans, adepts in the school-book field, have entered this software market, as have Macmillan Education in a deal with Sinclair Research. Books about computers and micros are also pouring on to the market from Michael Joseph (*The Fifth Generation* by Edward Feigenbaum and Pamela McCorduck no less), the Harvester Press, Century, Heinemann, Chapman & Hall and many others. Some elucidate the machines themselves, others explain how to choose for the home and a huge number give advice to businessmen. The National Computing Centre also runs its own line in publications. There is a new little income for publishers and authors in all this – the 'Compu-novel rights', a nice example of copyright's infinite divisibility.

## *Auctions*

Money, Tolstoy maintained, is compressed violence. It is also an expression of power, and the Chief Editor or, if the sum is big enough, the President or Managing Director, is at his most macho when in the heat of a book auction, especially in New York where the site can spread to the streets. I overheard the rumour that Mark Jaffe (then Chief Executive of Bantam and now of Villard books) had paid $2.8m for the paperback rights of Ed Doctorow's *Ragtime* in a restaurant off Wall Street not frequented by publishers. Everybody involved in an auction knows that they will have to pay more for the book than it can possibly earn.

Or will they? A sort of magic enters the scene. The internal morale of a successful publishing house is boosted. The battle and the victor make the *New York Times* and the London *Times* diary (at least). Trade sits up. When Anthony Cheetham (q.v.) bought the rights to *The Thorn Birds*, an Australian saga by Colleen McCullough (without the Australian rights, which were held by the original publishers, Harper & Row – like selling *Gone With the Wind* without rights for the southern states), for the Futura imprint of which he was progenitor, people, especially the unsuccessful bidders, thought he was mad or that he was so cross with his employers that he was looking for a way to bankrupt the company. Two

ears later he told me that almost every book in the Futura
st had lost money except *The Thorn Birds*. In the last stages
f a high-powered and well-conducted book auction, anybody
f consequence in the New York book world is literally and
etaphorically 'out to lunch'. Publishing rights are auctioned
y an agent. Mort Janklow – the subject of a *New Yorker*
eries – and Scott Meredith, possibly the cleverest literary
gent in the world (who recently boasted, when he received
n honorary degree, that he left school at the age of four),
re adepts. In London Gillon Aitken and Ed Victor are the
hampions, although the retired head of Curtis Brown,
Graham Watson, was no mean hand. The technique, which
bounds in jargon, consists of first securing a 'floor', an offer
o which the auctioneer can return should the bids not come
n. Subsequent bids might include guarantees of 'topping
ights', meaning the licence to have another go. The auction
an be conducted by telephone or by letter but the date and
ime must be fixed and adhered to.

The auction of paperback rights by hardback publishers is
nore fun. Most dramatic is when the bidders gather in a hired
oom – the Waldorf, the Sherry Netherland or the Pierre –
he sealed letters are opened as the clock strikes twelve and
he waiters hover with napkin-smothered bottles of well-iced
hampagne.

It can go wrong. I sold a novel written by Alan Williams
alled *Shahmak*, about the death of the Shah, to Pat Soliman,
who later became the first woman president of her publishing
ouse, Coward McCann Geoghegan. Only one person turned
p out of the rain to the auction to share her champagne and
e offered just $1,500, a fraction of what Pat had been hoping
or.

## *Book clubs*

Not everybody in the Western world has easy access to a
ookshop, especially in America. And not everybody, es-
ecially in America, can decide which books to buy. The book
lub is devised to fill these lacunae. Before 1966 the regulations

governing the way book clubs operate laid down that boo
club editions could not appear until nine months after th
'net' – i.e. price maintained – editions had been on sale in th
bookshops. In that year the Publishers Association Counc
agreed to the introduction of 'simultaneous' book clubs, s
that book club editions could appear, at a lower price, at th
same time as the trade editions. So now book club member
who undertake various continuing commitments to purchas
choices – the estimated 1.3 million members of Book Clu
Associates, founded in 1966 and owned jointly by W. H
Smith and Doubleday New York (it was based on the phenom
enally successful Literary Guild in America), the 400,00
members of Leisure Circle, started in 1978, and the 275,00
members of Reader's Union – can buy on publication, throug
their club, at the price of £5.50 a book that will cost everybod
else £6.95. A good popular wheeze, *pace* Bryan Forbes (q.v.
The book club argument (which prevailed) is that they spen
so much money exposing titles (Book Club Associates £
million in 1982) that generally speaking the trade as a who
benefits. The above are the three main clubs operating in th
UK. Leisure Circle are the most recent and, in that they hav
claimed to have discovered a new market for books, the mos
interesting.

When Herr Mohn of Gütersloh, Westphalia, travels on th
Autobahn he is accompanied at a discreet height by a polic
helicopter, for he is a most valuable member of the Federa
Republic. To be precise, at 63 he owns 82 per cent of Ber
telsmann, an international media company with a turnove
in 1981 of £1.6bn and a profit of £28m per annum. Ber
telsmann is second to Time-Life in the world media busines
They own two imprints in Germany, 100 per cent of Banta
and Corgi, and twenty-six book and record clubs througho
the world with a total of 15 million subscribers. For goo
measure Bertelsmann also owns *Der Stern* of the *Hitler Diarie*
fiasco and the prestigious magazine *Geo*. Book clubs form
huge proportion of Bertelsmann's profits and British ope
ations use the technique patented by Herr Mohn, who con
ceived the idea of door-to-door selling for book clubs whils
a prisoner-of-war in America. Agents, quite often scho

leavers, are assigned areas where they call on a door-to-door basis, deliver their (well-rehearsed) spiel to the householder and leave their literature; colourful stuff which covers a spectrum of mid- to downmarket publishing from Judith Guest and Laurence Olivier's autobiography to, not all that soft, porn. (They had a letter from an old age pensioner complaining that there were not enough bondage scenes in one of them: 'I am a lonely old man and I find bondage very comforting.')

The potential subscriber who commits him or herself to buying one book a quarter for a minimum of two years is then screened. The operation is profitable only after two years because the costs of the first sell are so high. Leisure Circle is run by Conrad Goulden (the son of Mark, who used to own W. H. Allen) and 190 employees.

With one assistant he alone buys the titles, about 250 of them a year. He relies entirely on his own judgment and has successfully reissued in hardback books like *Forever Amber*, *The Naked and the Dead*, *Peyton Place* and *The Exorcist* which have been long available at a lower price in paperback. The staple diet for members of this book club is middle-of-the-road fiction to which they would not otherwise have easy access.

'My members', says Conrad Goulden, 'feel awkward in bookshops.' Again, alas, as with public libraries, the only people who do not benefit from this expansion in the consumption of literature, in the loosest sense of the word, are the authors. Say a book club orders in advance 2,000 copies of a novel like *Golden Hill* by Shirley Lord from Frederick Muller, the publisher benefits by this top-up of his print-run which lowers the unit price and helps his net profit; but the author gets only a small percentage of the price received, otherwise the deal is simply not on. Despite protest from authors, agents, bookshops, the Writers' Guild and the Society of Authors, this arrangement seems likely to endure (although the book club's exclusive rights on a cheap edition of a title has been modified by a recent agreement).

Most publishers give their authors 10 per cent of the book club proceeds which might come out at, say, 14p per book.

Book clubs are now saying, however, that they would like even cheaper prices, perhaps 8,000 copies at £1.44p each, so that they can compete with paperbacks and yet cover their own high promotional costs. As the cost of book production does not diminish, the only way publishers can do this is to give even less to their authors. Publishers are loath to forgo the extra book club print run which helps their costs. They also value book club advertising and good media exposure of a title, so authors may have to accept this cut in income.

The book clubs bring middle of brow reading material to middle of brow people. They are no help to Literature, being tuned more to the Lowest Common Multiple than the Highest Uncommon Factor. All attempts to market High Lit. through book clubs have failed, the last being the estimable David Hughes's efforts, with the New Fiction Society, supported by the Literature Panel of the Arts Council.

# VIII *Production and printing*

Publishing pre-dates printing; a library of papyri was a status symbol for a rich Roman and could be numbered in thousands. Juvenal, asked by a friend for a copy of his satires, crossly directed his friend to his publisher. There was a street in Rome, rather like Paternoster Row in London before it was bombed, where publishers hung out, employing scribes, often Greek slaves, as copyists. The Letters of Paul, chronologically the first of the New Testament writers, were duplicated in this way throughout the Roman world. Papyrus is a reed and manuscripts were written on this material, or more grandly on vellum made from the inside of a sheep's skin. Paper was first developed in the second century by the Chinese, who used bamboo, mulberry and other native fibres. Not until 1085 did paper arrive in Europe as a result of the Moors' invasion of Spain. By the end of the thirteenth century a mill was established in Fabriano, Italy, where advanced techniques for making excellent paper by hand were developed. An inexpensive type of paper was essential to the successful development of printing and this came about when rags became the raw material for the new industry. Printing did not really get off the ground until people were rich enough to discard their rags. The city of Prato, near Florence, was the medieval centre for the rag trade, as Iris Origo explains in *The Merchant of Prato*.

Because of the time and effort required by hand-lettering,

books were scarce until the latter half of the fifteenth century. Then Gutenberg realized that he needed a method by which he could make impressions of type on paper. In 1438 he commissioned a cabinet-maker, Konrad Saspoch, to make a press to his specifications, adapting the wooden screw press already used for flattening sheets of paper and pressing grapes to make wine. These presses were copied throughout Europe and formed the basis of all printing until the appearance of high-speed presses in the mid-nineteenth century. But even then the process did not change greatly; Caxton would still have recognized what was being done. Being a gentleman, he did not operate the machines himself but left that to Wynkyn de Worde. Incidentally, Caxton had many more problems to contend with than today's printer, for he was translator, editor and publisher at a time when the language of spoken common English varied greatly from shire to shire so that he had to decide which term and words to use and how to spell them. As he himself said in his preface to *Eneydos*, which he translated from a French version of Virgil's *Aeneid*, 'Certainly it is hard to please every man . . . Therefore I have reduced and translated this said book into our English, not overrude, nor curious but in such terms as shall be understood, by God's grace, according to my copy.' Not only is the language and spelling of English standardized today, which helps, but there have been several revolutions in printing since Caxton.

Today publishers do not write or sell the books, nor usually do they print them. In Britain, only a few houses, e.g. Oxford and Cambridge and Collins (in Glasgow), have printing shops.

Publishers with very little capital apart from their office equipment can lose their heads, pay far too much for a book, print far too many and sell far too few. This trap must be avoided by the wily publisher. The trouble is that, while at the moment of acquisition a property, like a potential Derby winner, may seem to be on winning form, in between contract and publication the animal develops asthma, or it becomes clear that the publisher has overestimated its stamina.

Unfortunately, the kind of self-induced optimism, amounting sometimes to hysteria, which produces such grandiose advances and print orders is infectious, and there has yet to be a printer who has quietly offered doubts as to the wisdom of spoiling so many tons of clean white paper with so many gallons of ink. A wise publisher should remember, first, that it is always possible to reprint a book running well, and, second, that no publisher ever went broke on the books he *didn't* print (though with a fashionable, fast-thinking title with a short selling life he might lose profit by going early out of print).

The design and appearance of a general book matter, but not too much; after all, printing is only a form of communication and rarely an end in itself. A book should be readable and clean, and the design should not obtrude to the extent that it distracts the reader from the author's thoughts.

After all, as my late-lamented mentor, Antony Gibbs, said to his equally late (and faintly lamentable) partner, Charles Fry, who was fussing about the appearance of a book, 'Nobody ever returns a book to a shop complaining that it is printed in Baskerville 11/12 instead of Bembo 14.'

However, in the last decade the public has been tuned to expect that a certain kind of biography or non-book be presented in jazzy, variegated, visual form and the success of books like Patrick Marnham's *The Private Eye Story* or a funny like *DIY Brain Surgery* proves they like it. Such antics are best left to packagers.

Doug Bristow, ex-Managing Director of Hazell Watson and Viney, recalls that when he worked as a lad in a publisher's office, the author's royalty book was known as the 'GL' – the gentlemen's ledger. There are no gentlemen's ledgers in print factories.

## *Preparation of copy for press*

Whilst the manuscript is still in the publishing house, it will be sent to the copy-editing department, where the typescript is carefully checked for errors, spelling and punctuation. It is then marked up by the designer for typesetting to show size of typeface and kind, layout of opening pages, chapter headings and any special peculiarities.

It then passes into the hands of the production department. Production people are responsible for getting the finished object into the warehouse in time for publication. This involves booking space at the typesetter's, printer's and binder's, ordering the necessary paper, costing, liaising with the editor (and possibly author) over proof dates, and so on. They send the manuscript to the typesetter.

The manuscript of this book, having been subjected to all the foregoing processes, was sent to Rowland Phototypesetting Ltd. The first operation is casting off. This means counting the number of words per page to calculate how long the finished book will be because on this information all the manufacturing costs can be estimated. If a cast-off and estimate have already been done in the publishing house it is as well, time permitting, to have it checked.

The manuscript will then proceed to copy preparation, where, depending upon the system of composition being used, it will be marked with the appropriate codes.

## *Typesetting*

Apart from a few private presses which still set in hot metal, virtually all commercial composition is now photographic – this is the revolution. There are many different machines and the number appears to be getting larger every day. They can, however, be broken down into two groups. The first and oldest are the machines such as Monophoto and VIP (Variable Input Phototypesetter). These shine a light through a matrix negative in the shape of the letter on to film or bromide paper. The second and more common group uses digitized typefaces, held on floppy disk; these either transmit the typeface on to a cathode ray tube or guide a laser beam directly on to the film or paper. Film is being superseded by photographic paper, which is easier to handle.

In any event the compositor who now sits in front of a modern keyboard will type almost continually, keying in the awkward bits, e.g. footnotes, space for illustrations, changes of typeface and/or size, with special command keys at the same time. This character 'string' can be held either on floppy disk or tape and drives either a line printer or the photosetter itself. A photosetter will have an H & J program (hyphenation and justification) and can perform automatic page make-up, photostatting pages exactly as they will appear in the final printed form.

After the proofs have been read and corrected, the pages containing corrections are usually called back from the disk or tape to a VDU (Visual Display Unit) screen and the correction recorded. The correction can then be made either by resetting the whole page or by the less efficient, but possibly cost-effective method of resetting one line and sticking it down (stripping in) over the incorrect line.

The majority of automatic page make-up systems work only with relatively simple pages and therefore multiple-column pages need to be made up by hand from correctly set galleys. This is commonly done with scalpel and glue over a lightbox and a grid. As it involves a lot of hand work it is more expensive. There are some page make-up systems which will handle this type of work on a screen. At present these tend to be high-priced but costs will doubtless be reduced.

Where space has been left in the pages for illustrations these can be handled either by photographing the original illustration and combining the illustration film with the film of the page, or by PMT (photo mechanical transfer). This is a method of producing a screened print suitable for sticking into the page in order that it can be photographed at the same time as the text. Frontispieces are *out* as they normally have to be inserted by hand. Today it costs more to insert a frontispiece than to put in a single section.

The page is then photographed. If there are illustration films to be combined they will be combined now. This results in a piece of negative film which can either be used directly for making the printing plates or can be contacted to positive film if positive plates are to be used.

This procedure, which could be called medium high-tech, is simpler, cheaper, quicker and cleaner than the letterpress method which involved pernickety fiddling with tweezers and tiny ems and ens (good words for Scrabble). The modern comp (ositor) wears an M & S cashmere woolly and has clean fingernails; his grandad was inky-fingered in an overall and being a Methodist lay preacher on the side refused to type words like f***. However, in due course there will probably be another revolution when the first typing of all manuscripts will be done in the publisher's office and edited on a VDU, or the author will type into a word processor and send the disk to the publisher, who will edit again on his or her VDU, insert photosetter commands for typeface, style, etc., and merely send the disk to their chosen supplier who has the actual typesetting device. It will be DIY in the electronic home office. The corrections to Arthur C. Clarke's latest work were transmitted to New York from Sri Lanka by satellite.

## *Printing*

Because of the high capital cost of printing technology much research has gone into making machines run faster and faster. In the end offset lithography, commonly known as 'offset' or 'litho', has taken over. Not only do these presses run much faster than old letterpress machines, but they take less time to set up and use less energy.

The principle on which they work is that grease and water do not mix. Each press will have one or more litho plates printing either one or both sides of a sheet. The image of the words has been photographically transferred on to this plate and accepts ink – which is greasy – but not water. As the plate revolves it is first moistened by a damping roller which dampens the plate around the image area. This is then followed by the inking roller; the ink will not stick to the damp plate but sticks to the image which has no water on it. The sheet of paper then goes through and comes out the other end of the machine beautifully printed. If the machine prints one side only it is called a single-sided machine whereas if it prints both sides at once it is called a 'perfector'. This is from the old printing jargon wherein a sheet printed on the second side was considered 'perfect'.

Printing presses now come in two varieties: 'sheet-fed', where the paper is passed through in individual sheets, and 'reel', where it goes through on a continuous reel – much quicker and cheaper. The 1970s saw the advent of 'mini-webs', originally converted newspaper presses, now manufactured specially for book printing. Apart from running faster, paper on a reel can be folded by running it over angled folding bars and the folded sections thus formed can be quickly separated by an automatic cutter at the end of the machine. This eliminates the need for a separate folding operation and saves costs.

## *Binding*

When the sheets come from the end of the printing machine they will be folded to form sections or 'signatures'. The elegant simplicity of the metric system – the largest sheet of paper is one metre square, called A0 (based on the pure Greek triangle which is always in proportion however many times you fold it). All other sizes are fractions of A0. A4 for instance is one-sixteenth. Take a piece of paper, fold it in half, fold it across the middle again and yet again across the middle and you will end up with a small pad; number each page and then unfold it – you will find numbers scattered *apparently* indiscriminately over the sheet. This is the way the pages are placed on the printing plate in order that *after* folding the book will read consecutively. Sections can be in sixteens, twenty-fours or thirty-twos. There are others but these are the most common and are all based on multiples of eight. The page you are reading is page 15 of section 5.

After folding, the sections must be gathered and collated, which simply means that they are put together in order, with section one at the front and section whatever at the end.

At this point binding methods will diverge. The first divergence is between sewing and what has unhappily been called 'perfect' binding, which is now more commonly known as 'unsewn'. If the book is to be sewn the sheets will be sent first to an endpapering machine and then to the sewing machine, which will sew them continuously with one book actually attached to the next. These will then be separated and sent to the binding line.

Assuming a cased book (hardback), the cases have by this time been made and blocked with the title on the spine. The book 'block' is 'lined', which means placing some form of reinforcing material – gauze called 'mull' in the good old days – around the spine and slightly overlapping the endpaper. (If you look at the endpaper stuck to the board of any cased book you will see a raised edge near the spine.) Following this, top, fore-edge and bottom are neatly trimmed by a three-knife trimmer to remove folded edges and to separate the pages. The book is then placed in its case after undergoing a variety of processes, all of which are designed to ensure that it holds together. The main processes are 'rounding and backing', which puts the curve in the front and spine, and 'nipping', which puts the neat shoulders down the spine. From here the book will go to the jacketing machine where the pre-printed jacket will be put on it. Jackets (q.v.) prepared ahead of the book sometimes don't fit – a common publisher's nightmare.

With an unsewn book the spines of the folded sections are roughly cut off and glue applied to hold the pages together. From here the book can be bound as an unsewn cased book with a lining or, more likely, as one operation it will be fed into a wrappering machine, which will put a cover on it to turn it into a paperback.

## *Paper*

This book is printed on a paper called Ganton Antique Wove. For books of this type the standard paper used is an antique wove. It is produced (as are all papers with the exception of specialist papers) from wood pulp. Usually the wood pulp is imported from Scandinavia and converted in English paper mills to its final form. It will be called either 'wood *free*', which means only that it is chemically stewed to eliminate lignin, that component which causes paper to turn brown, or 'mechanical' (also known as ground wood), when the trees are mechanically ground to pulp. Without any chemical treatment this does not remove the lignin and the paper discolours readily, so mechanical papers are used mainly in mass-market paperback production, where the book has a limited shelf life. When the pulp reaches the paper mill it is passed through a machine called a hydropulper, which adds water and chemicals, reducing it to a very thin liquid. It is then passed through another machine called a beater, which, being rather like a turbine, makes the wood fibres feathery. A wood free paper, because it has not been ground, has longer fibres than a mechanical paper, where the fibres will have been broken. This then goes to the wet end of a paper-making machine where, with the addition of further chemicals, it is spread on to a wire mesh. Here the water drains out and the wet pulp consolidates to a mat. Wood free papers with their long fibres lock together far better than a short fibred mechanical paper. Also at the 'beating' stage the paper will be 'loaded' with various chemicals such as china clay (china clay is like dazzling white silk; it comes from Cornwall along with tin and was almost the first British export. Visitors to Charlestown might have noticed china clay glittering in the holds of little ships) and gypsum to increase its opacity and 'printability'. It then passes through sets of drying rollers and also through a set of rollers which will squeeze it to control its thickness or caliper. If it is an antique wove which is being made to a specific thickness or 'volume' these will be set to a specific distance. At the end of the paper-making machine the paper is reeled.

The variety of papers is enormous and the same paper from one mill may be sold by different merchants as well as direct from the mill under more than one trade name. It is advisable to acquire and label a set of papers from the supplier for reference. The subject is so complex that an aspiring all-rounder should attend a course and visit paper mills.

Novels, biographies, etc., these days are printed on antique wove paper in fairly small runs, which means that the amount of paper required would be below the minimum 'making' –

nowadays usually between two and five tonnes. If there is an illustration section printed on art paper this would almost certainly need to come from stock and is even better supplied by the printer.

Paper sizes are obviously dictated by the size of the book which in itself may be dictated by the size of the printing presses of the chosen printer, especially in the case of a mini-web.

Paper mills are highly automated and capital-intensive, costing millions to revamp. Harold Wilson was much criticized for subsidizing one of the mills, Fort William, owned by Wiggins Teape. However, a small publisher won't deal direct with the mill but probably through a paper merchant. A pity, as playing around with the unspoilt white samples is rather fun.

## *Paperbacks*

Only black ink is used in the paperback printing operation and, traditionally, the paper is reel-fed through a rotary letterpress machine. This machine prints either from rubber or photopolymer plates (plastic nylon material which incidentally is the more modern process and the plates last longer, they think, than rubber). Folded signatures are produced and they come in bundles of either 16/16, 20/20, 24/24 or 32/32. These are now ready for 2-up binding. The double-decker piles of signatures are gathered up according to the following formula – 1–8, 2–7, 3–6, 4–5, 5–4 . . . It's called 'coming and going' and should mean the final pages of the book turn up in the right sequence. The backs are then cut off and adhesives applied, the covers are glued on and the books shaped in a clamp. The final operation, when covered Siamese twins of books chunter down the belt, is that they are severed one from the other, the head, tail and fore-edge trimmed and pushed on to the world.

## *Hardbacks*

Most case-bound books (hardbacks) are printed by a litho process, either on sheet-fed offset presses or, in the event of black only, on heat-set monochrome web presses. When colour is required the colour printing goes in the following sequence: blue, yellow, red, black. This does not mean the sheets have to be fed through the machine four times in the case of a four-colour job: once is enough, as each unit in the machine is responsible for one colour and acts when instructed.

The next operation is to fold the sheets, attach endpapers to the first and last signatures and bind as described on p. 131. The final adornment is the jacket. Some grand books are then wrapped further in boxes or slip-cases but these are again made of board covered with cloth and glued together.

The people who work in a publisher's production department are generally as cautious and pessimistic as editors are incautious and optimistic. Book printers on the other hand can be quite jolly. Doug Bristow (see above) 'makes', as New Yorkers say, 'good lunch'. It took me two days to recover from his hospitality at the Bell at Aston Clinton.

# IX *Reviews*

A book is published every twenty minutes of the working day. Of a Thursday this can mean four hundred novels for the favour of reviews. How does an editor decide which shall be chosen? The posh Sundays (the phrase comes from *Look Back in Anger*, 1956) often all review the same titles. This leads the Dave Sparts to complain that they are corrupt, fascist and elitist. Corrupt they are not; as Jack Lambert said, 'Without sherry importers the *Sunday Times* book section would be bereft of advertisements.' Fascist, no. Even in the *Sunday Times*, a book of liberal tinge has a better chance than a monetarist, right-wing polemic: think of the fuss about Skidelsky's biography of John Maynard Keynes. Elitist, yes, but literary editors are journalists first and foremost and get paid to fill their columns with good copy. Elitists make good copy.

So does the literary editor send out for review those books which will make the liveliest journalism, those where the author's name seems familiar, those which are topical, or those which he feels would respond best to serious, trenchant criticism? To find an answer I wrote to A. N. Wilson, erstwhile literary editor of the *Spectator* and rising star in the literary firmament, winner of the John Llewelyn Rhys Prize for both *The Sweets of Pimlico* and for *The Laird of Abbotsford*, winner of the Southern Arts Literature Prize, the Arts Council National Book Award and the Somerset Maugham Award for his novel *The Healing Art*, and expert on John Milton. A. N. Wilson told me that he thought 'the days had vanished when reviewing was a "serious" matter. The articles in the Sunday papers are far too short to be able to do justice to a book. The *New Statesman* has collapsed, so has *The Times Literary Supplement*. Very occasionally one gets a good article in *The London Review of Books*. The *Spectator* has never, since the days of Mr Gladstone, made any claims to take literature seriously.'

> I think the book reviews of a paper, like any other section of it, should be lively and entertaining as journalism. When I was literary editor (the term hardly applies to the *Spectator*, but that was what they called me), I selected books for review which I thought would produce amusing articles from the reviewers. There is no such thing as a book which 'ought' to be reviewed. I was not influenced by letters from publishers, and I never knew until the book had been sent out for review, whether the publisher intended to spend money on my page advertising it or not. I do not think reviews are very 'important'. I do not think they can affect the sales of a book, and I hope that no one takes them very seriously.
>
> I think the book pages of a paper are considerably less important than the gossip column or the city pages; and considerably less interesting to most people than the sports pages; so it seems silly to make too much fuss about them. There are some publishers and literary editors who fail to realize that almost nobody *reads* these pages. This morning for example, I turned the pages of the *Telegraph* to see what Anthony Powell had chosen to review, but I will never read to the *end* of his article. I think most people are like me in this respect. I have hardly ever read to the end of a review, except the ones I was paid to 'sub'.

would disagree with him about the influence of reviews. The *Spectator*, for instance, may only have a tiny circulation but t is among people who can all afford to buy hardbacks and n the main do so frequently. Many of them rely on the

*Spectator* to help them to choose what they will buy when they next visit Hatchards, John Sandoe, Heywood Hill or the Belgravia Bookshop.

Terence Kilmartin, literary editor of the *Observer*, thinks that on occasion reviews can sell a book, and he instances *Hope Against Hope* by Nadezhda Mandelstam, which was translated from the Russian and published by Collins and the Harvill Press in England in March 1971.

> It got very well reviewed in the *Observer* and elsewhere as well. Then there was, what I have always regarded as being absurd, the annual game of the books of the year. When that was played in 1971, I had read *Hope Against Hope* and thought it was one of the greatest books in the world so when people who had been asked for their recommendations said to me, 'I don't seem to have read any books to put forward,' I said to them, 'Have you read *Hope Against Hope*?' Some said, 'Oh, marvellous book,' but two hadn't read it. Thirteen people out of thirty chose Mandelstam's book as their Book of the Year and that made it. It was deliberate on my part but it is the only time I can remember thinking 'this is such a great book one ought to cheat like mad so that people read it.'

Terry also pointed out that 'What people like reading on a Sunday is A. J. P Taylor writing a twelve hundred word essay on Bismarck.' He feels strongly that his reviewers are there to interest people in books, in buying them and in getting them out of the library. So I decided to analyse the literary sections of the posh papers on January 22nd, 1984 to see how helpful they were. It was an insignificant day, the main news being reactions to Enoch Powell's attack on the Queen's speech where, he said, she favoured a 'vociferous minority of newcomers', instead of more properly addressing herself to the British and Christian majority of her subjects.

The *Sunday Telegraph* reviewed nineteen hardback books (their colour magazine dealt with the paperbacks, chosen by Lady Selina Hastings). In one page they dealt with nine poets including a £55 volume of Wilfred Owen from the Hogarth

Press. A. N. Wilson wrote on *Arthur Ransome*, a biography from Cape; Auberon Waugh dealt with novels, and Bernard Levin's essays were reviewed, another Cape book. The two lives of Dashiell Hammett were reviewed by Gavin Lyall.

The *Sunday Times* reviewed eight hardbacks and nine paperbacks. One life of Hammett was reviewed, so was *Arthur Ransome*. A book about Zinoviev (Gollancz) was reviewed by Ferdy Mount, lives of Bunuel and Polanski were reviewed by Peter Ackroyd. A big biography on Carlyle and two volumes of autobiography of Storm Jameson from Virago were also there.

Over two pages the *Observer* reviewed twenty-four books. It included a life of Bunuel and Anthony Burgess on two Hammett biographies. Five period novels were reviewed by Stephen Vaughan, led by the *Oxherder's Tale* – one of our books. Another five novels were reviewed by Anthony Thwaite, and Martin Amis had unkind things to say about Heinemann's biography of Polanski, 'a tribute to the searing power of the cliché . . . inanimate, affectless, half-engaged'. Bernard Williams chuntered on about Bertrand Russell's diary, one of many colossal volumes.

Big-name publishers predominated: a lot of Cape, Allen & Unwin, Heinemann, Chatto, Hamish Hamilton and Sidgwick & Jackson. Odd absentees were Weidenfeld & Nicolson, commonly review-scoopers. All the books and the reviewers were from the Establishment. One would have thought the three posh papers might have had different attitudes. But no. Just a typical dull Sunday afternoon, nothing new, nothing scandalous, nothing electric.

Of the books considered, the most successful must have been Germaine Greer's new work, serialized in the *Sunday Times*. Of the long reviews, most will have served as a substitute for buying the book. Only a tiny fraction of the books published that week would have been mentioned and those that were, were safe, predictable and expensive. Minority fiction gets more space than a new Irving Wallace, so does minority non-fiction. Children get a look-in at Christmas and perhaps once again during the year; more space is given to crime and detection than to science fiction or poetry.

Philip Howard, literary editor of *The Times*, suggested in his paper that reviewers should produce lively journalism and serious criticism when called upon to do so, although there was little time in the hurly-burly of daily journalism with its tight schedules and harsh deadlines. 'To write a proper review of an important book, which the author may have spent a lifetime writing, is a serious, rather an awesome business. One could spend a whole week, a month, three months, on doing it justice . . . but there comes a time when you must stop rewriting and polishing, and deliver the right number of words, even though they are not perfect.'

Barbed reviews are good for declamation only: every schoolboy knows Lord Macaulay's piece on Mr Robert Montgomery's poems ('His writing bears the same relation to poetry which a Turkey carpet bears to a picture . . . readers must take such grammar as they can get, and be thankful'). They don't sell books. But controversial reviews may encourage people to find out the truth for themselves. Certainly when two books are reviewed together, one well, one badly, few remember which book received which reception by the time they have walked to the bookshop. The author will remember.

Today no one person can make a book in the way Arnold Bennett is said to have been able to do, although Bron Waugh can be instrumental in so doing. But this is not accomplished by articles dripping with 'fulsome honey and flowers' for these are more often than not unreadable and unread. But, 'Be careful how you cross the road Mr Bellow,' shouted by the *Daily Express*, 'we love you!' certainly moved *Herzog*.

Reviewers do not like being quoted out of context, nor do they care to see the odd complimentary word splashed in scarlet across a jacket when they remember full well that the main tenor of their comment was lukewarm, but a book may die if it is not swiftly attended to and a small puff or endorsement can be the kiss of life. Even a brief mention on *The Times* back-page list can keep it gasping.

Who are these practitioners of first-aid? For the most part they come from the groves of academe or have themselves written eye-catching literary works of some kind. Martin

Amis, Kingsley's son, gained a starred first at Oxford, wrote to Terry Kilmartin and was given a chance to prove himself. Philip French's son Sean was also allowed to have a go in the *Sunday Times*, having gained a first. On the whole, reviewers seem to be mildly middle-class, cliquey junior dons and junior novelists who keep going year after year. Some are paid on salary, others by the word – usually about £10 a hundred. There are a few who are under contract for so many pieces a year, for so much money which is fixed in advance: Anthony Burgess, for instance, gets at least £300 a throw. He was once literary editor of the *Yorkshire Post* but praised a novel he had written under a pseudonym. The *Post* was not amused. London was and he was made.

The *Yorkshire Post* is one of the most influential newspapers outside London, others are the *Glasgow Herald*, the *Western Morning News*, *Eastern Daily Press*, *Oxford Mail*, *Scotsman*, the *Liverpool Echo* and the *Birmingham Post*, which gives a Christmas pudding to every old age pensioner in the city. All these newspapers have lively and highly effective literary editors. An interesting new phenomenon is the reviewing power of the free newspapers like *The Magazine*, shoved through letter boxes in Belgravia and trendy NW1, who often support quite high-powered hacks.

And the other literary editors? Terence Kilmartin, translator of Proust and Montherlant, is the doyen, having been chosen for the *Observer* by David Astor decades ago; Claire Tomalin, Cambridge first and author of a biography of Mary Wollstonecraft, is at the *Sunday Times*; Philip Howard has succeeded Ion Trewin at *The Times*; Christopher Hudson, now writing the book after-the-film-has-been-made-by-David Puttnam, is at the *Standard*; W. L. (Bill) Webb has been at the *Guardian* for years; the *New Statesman* has declined like the party it supports; the *Spectator*'s literary editorship is a hot and fashionable seat: it has been occupied in turn by Ferdinand Mount, Patrick Marnham, A. N. Wilson, Patrick Marnham and Ferdy Mount over the last two years. Anthony Curtis (brother John is at Weidenfeld) has been at the *Financial Times* since he left the *Sunday Telegraph* in the mid-1970s and Nicholas Bagnall and David Holloway have run the

*Telegraph*'s book pages for yonks. None of them can be fixed.

Some of these literary editors take notice of publishers' letters, if they do not write too often; others don't, sickened by puffs and circulars, roneo-ed personal letters and over-hyping: a good deal of this publicity seems to backfire. But most editors have sharp antennae, attend publishers' parties, hear what is in the wind and watch out for new works by the well-known. In particular they admit to watching literary imprints with care. Over two hundred hardbacks may arrive in their offices in any one week but Terence Kilmartin said that Cape, Deutsch, Chatto and Faber all have good track records so that he would be likely to pick out one of their books for a quick glance. New publishers, such as Michael Russell, must sell themselves for a bit when they are only just beginning.

What if a badly printed book from an unknown imprint appears which eventually turns out to be the next earth-mover after *Das Kapital*? Would it get reviewed? That seems unlikely. Very unlikely if it is a scientific book, for they seldom get noticed in the posh papers. The best such a book could hope for would be a brief mention by *The Times* in its column of interesting books received that week.

Several papers carry occasional odd lists of books received or shortlists of selected titles of one kind or another and most newspapers, as opposed to periodicals, mention the bestsellers on their book review page. Some print in all the non-books like the *F-Plan Diet*, the book of the television series or the *Guinness Book of Records*, which made millionaires out of the McWhirter twins. References to feats of eating and drinking are now out, since it was discovered people were literally killing themselves to get into the book.

The *Sunday Telegraph* sensibly annotates its list, calling it 'Books most in demand' and takes the trouble to state clearly which bookshops were asked for their opinions when the list was being compiled. Lists of the best books of the year, lists of this or that may seem somewhat ludicrous but they generate debate, gain publicity for books and stimulate arguments about books as a subject, encouraging people to visit their local bookshops and libraries. The publishing publicity machine and trade pressure groups like the Book Marketing Council have received flak from such pundits as Bernard Levin and Paul Johnson for their efforts to run circuses and competitions for the best young writer, or the best twelve novelists in England since 1945, because the pundits feel such goings-on are unworthy of literature. Maybe. But they are not unworthy of the book *trade*.

# X *Selling and publicity*

I used to have a special sheet which I distributed to first-time authors entitled 'Why your book is not at Didcot Station'. It began by examining the operation of W. H. Smith, the biggest booksellers and wholesalers in England, as opposed to Scotland (which is dominated by Menzies), to find out why. Supposing you have read an interesting review in the *Spectator* of a novel called *The Masque of St Eadmundsburg* by Humphrey S. Morrison, published by Blond & Briggs. You enter a branch of W. H. Smith anywhere from Andover to Zeals with the sincere intention of purchasing a copy for your favourite aunt who is being dried out in Weston-super-Mare. If you enunciate too clearly the title, author, publisher and price the assistant will suspect quite properly that you are the author or his mother.

The branch will not have a copy in stock (head office out of the kindness of its heart will have ordered twenty-five copies), in fact, it is easier to buy a typewriter or a video cassette of your choice in a W. H. Smith than the book you want. Any W. H. Smith branch will stock dictionaries from Collins and OUP, Teach Yourself books, Beatrix Potter, the latest diet book and in paperback the latest Robbins, Archer, Higgins etc., for a very good reason. They sell. W. H. Smith have some up-market shops under their own name, notably their splendid branch in Sloane Square, and own others such as Truslove & Hanson, Bowes & Bowes in Cambridge and

Sherratt & Hughes in Manchester, but they cannot be expected to stock more than a minute fraction of the 5,000-odd fiction titles publishers persist in flooding into a stagnant market. They will, however, take your order which will, eventually, result in the book being despatched to the branch either direct from the publisher's warehouse or via Smith's headquarters in Swindon.

The single-copy order, as it is known, is the bane of the book trade, complicated, tedious and unprofitable. Simplifying the process has defied the genius of even Captain Robert Maxwell, who went broke trying to do so in the 1950s, and though they now use tele-ordering, which can reduce the time taken to as little as five days (see Bryan Forbes), publishers and booksellers have not yet agreed on standard orders, standard discounts or standard anything. A publisher's order department has to process daily orders which vary in size from a Buster Keaton-style computer print-out a yard long with only two lines on it, to orders from Basil Blackwell so handsome that they resemble a writ, to strips of confetti from Holland (which incidentally has the most efficient book distribution in the world). This confusion, compounding frustration and expense, seems insoluble. You can't be blamed for only wanting one copy of *The Masque of St Eadmundsburg*, the assistant in Smith's ditto for not having heard of it, nor the publisher, who thought he was making a contribution to literature, for not having printed a bestseller. It is to be hoped that your aunt takes some time to dry out.

Books in their inception, production and distribution cannot be hurried. Dr Johnson solicited subscribers in order to finance his dictionary and in the eighteenth century their names were often listed in the resulting book. Books are still subscribed by the publisher's sales representatives: with anxious expressions and bulky bags full of the publisher's seasonal wares, they trek round the bookshops. In London they are expected to hump a final copy of each title, but in the country they just carry the jackets. The modest old subfusc dustcover has now graduated into a glossy which, because it is the publisher's main publicity thrust, often rates a department of its own, certainly in paperback houses where the jacket can cost more than the author's advance. It was always mooted that one of the many reasons why Allen Lane fired his managing editor, Tony Godwin, was that he (successfully) changed Penguin's colour-banded covers, green for thrillers, orange for fiction, etc., into more ambitious pictorial representations.

A jacket is the first intimation to the bookselling trade of the imminence of a new title and in the case of library suppliers, it is all anyone there will ever see of the book. The rule of thumb obtaining is that 700 jackets must be distributed to potential buyers in the United Kingdom and the Commonwealth, the further in advance of publication the better, which is one of the reasons why books should not be *hurried*. No publisher has ever been sued, at least by the trade, for delaying publication and the longer the jacket is around in the folders of representatives throughout the world, the more it will garner in 'subscriptions'. A jacket can be a single-colour design like *The Establishment*, which was my first successful book, or a five-colour printing of *The Fourth of June*, my first successful novel. The message should above all be clear. Too clever, too subtle, too complicated, even too beautiful a jacket may miss the mark. I once published a book on lunacy called *The Moon is Full* with a lovely scraperboard drawing by Illingworth of a moon staring through the bars of a bin; nevertheless it was thought to be a work on astronomy. However, jackets can be fun and even occasionally smack of genius, like that on *Papillon*, a padlock and a butterfly. The publishers of, say, Le Carré, will know that the author is their unique selling point and display his name with appropriate emphasis, no need for a pretty picture: the publishers of an unknown first novel have another problem.

Printed on the inside front flap of the jacket is the blurb: the product of much toil. It must appeal to, in this order, the bookseller, the reviewer and the browser in the bookshop. Ideally the first paragraph, which is as far as most people will go, should summarize the reasons for publishing the book. There is an absurd convention that the back flap should reveal a glamorous photograph of the author taken at his most alluring, displayed over a few trite phrases about his house near Guildford, his Swiss wife and two children. Alastair Maclean fitted this bill precisely; success drove him later to Switzerland. Jackets are crucial and can make or break a book.

'In selling books aggression should be used sparingly,' says Peter Stern, who for twenty-five years represented the Heinemann Group in London, visiting large, small, general and specialized bookshops as well as library suppliers.

> The selling of books is as much about people as it is about books. If the representative does not build up a mutual trust and confidence with those to whom he has to sell, he had better do something else. It takes more time than one might think to do this and even more than some are able to give: for in London the representative must be able to complete his 'talk' – pinpointing one or two salient features – in about two minutes.
>
> Out of the fifteen or twenty titles on a given publisher's list taken round every month, there will usually be two or three that the representative or the publisher (preferably both) feel strongly about. With these he must go out with all guns firing. He must know the book inside out and all about the author, his previous books, where he lives and what he does. He must also know exactly what publicity is available for important titles so he can offer to set up displays or dress a window whenever he gets the chance. When this combined operation between publisher, representative and bookseller really works, it is a fascinating enterprise to be concerned with, but to be successful needs immense effort and diplomacy.
>
> There are occasions when even though a representative may have confidence in a book and feel strongly about its potential, it does not strike the right chord with the buyer. I remember one which I was taking round many years ago, which illustrates this point. It was an historical book by an important American [William Shirer's *The Rise and Fall of the Third Reich*] and I felt strongly that it ought to do well at London Airport. I arrived there early one morning, full of hope, but nothing I could say would convince the buyer

of my enthusiasm. 'Pete,' he said, 'it's too academic, too
long, too heavy. Who on earth is going to take that on a
aeroplane? It's not for us.' In the end he said, 'Send u
three, we'll see what happens. Just 'cos it's you, mind.
They sold over 1,500 copies there alone in the space of les
than five months. In the early stages I had a job to get them
there fast enough.

With some buyers the last thing you'd talk about wa
books. I remember one bookseller I called on regularl
always discussed lawnmowers with me.

In the muddled, hectic, chaos-seeming world of book
sellers, it is the representative who has the unenviable tas
of building up a relationship of trust with the buyer whils
at the same time continuing to keep the publisher to th
fore.

The salesman is the linchpin between publisher and writer -
bookshop and reader: he is crucial to the whole sales oper
ation. What is more, he must get it right first time round
otherwise next time he visits, the unsold books he pressure
the buyer into taking will be sitting there in a pile to moc
him: trust will have tarnished.

In return for getting the rep to stick his neck out, th
publisher should back him up with a good, professional trad
counter which gets the orders out fast, should make sure h
has all the special material he needs and has plenty to show
the bookseller in good time.

The overseas representative selling English books in Europe
India, Africa and Asia has an even more difficult task an
needs to possess even greater skills, including languages an
knowledge of the country he is in. Uli Bruno, of Harper &
Row Europe, always takes a prospective representative ou
for a three-course meal before employing him or her 'becaus
you can discover a lot from the way a person tackles a bone'
He feels that his representatives are front-line diplomats fo
the firm, receiving and giving information and filtering thei
huge, complex list through to the right shop and so to th
ultimate user. Unfortunately the job used to attract what h
calls 'young freshmen from College or University, who woul

do a modern version of sowing wild oats by travelling for a publisher – often in a rather Wodehousian way.' These young men would learn on the job, to the anger of the booksellers. Two years later, oats sowed, market knowledge gained, they would move on to become sales managers. Now Uli Bruno tries to see that they are trained before they start out on their journeys for him.

Catalogues and backlists need interpreting for foreign customers who want to know exactly what is in the book, and why they should buy it. The bookseller doesn't want to give a firm order for a full-colour medical atlas, say, only to find when it arrives that it is in black and white. Representatives must be fully informed, honest, well-mannered and diplomatic. This way they build up a useful relationship with the buyer, who in turn will pass information about his customers' needs back.

Feedback straight from the horse's mouth, from schoolteachers, librarians and booksellers in a foreign country, is of immense value for it is far more accurate knowledge than that gleaned from local journals, back numbers of *The Economist* or bought market research. New data can enable the publisher to tailor his efforts and modify his programme in that country if need be – particularly useful in the case of school textbooks.

Good representatives are gold-dust and are cherished as such with the publisher's sales force endeavouring to back them to the hilt. Even so, German booksellers have an annual *Verlegerbeschimpfung*, or scold-the-publisher session: all too often claiming that the representatives lie and offer terms they cannot keep.

What representatives and bookshops look forward to is a book backed by a great deal of publicity on radio and television, in gossip columns in the weeklies and dailies, right across the board. But all too often the only publicity achieved by most titles is a listing in the back of the *Bookseller* and *Publishers Weekly* which gives in small type the book's title, author, price, pages, publisher, ISBN number and its category in the Library of Congress Catalog. After all, what else does one need to say about *Contributions to the Ecology of Halophytes*? Further, since only about 6,000 of the 40,000 books

British publishers perversely pump into the marketplace a year get reviewed, it must be assumed that the others find their small audience through different means (or should never have been published at all).

No publisher, however much they pretend in the trade press, can afford a campaign for every title. A 'hype' costs money and the decision of which book to favour is the first agony. Obviously, if a big advance has been paid, say as a result of winning an auction (q.v.), the matter decides itself and the hype is on. Or, an agent might have insisted contractually on x thousand pounds being spent on publicity with a no-nonsense clause about invoices having to be produced. Sometimes it doesn't work. *The Four Hundred*, agented by Ed Victor (q.v.), is a sensational example of the hype that failed. *The Day the Bubble Burst* was a pre-validated, computered success which almost didn't work. The second version of *The Country Diary of an Edwardian Lady*, published in America by Holt, Rinehart & Winston in a cheap trade edition, can now be bought in tens of thousands for a few cents. But the publishers bat on. They have to.

A book must first be sold 'in-house' and then to the trade, for the public buy books from a bookseller, not from the media. The publisher's sales representative must be turned-on in-house by the sales and publicity departments. The author of a big title will be asked to attend a sales conference to endear himself to the people who will be selling the product. It helps if a rep can tell a bookshop buyer in Wigan that he shared a Martini with the author and that he's a nice guy.

The hero of *Something Happened*, a novel by Joseph Heller, author of *Catch-22*, is obsessed by the fear that he may *not* be chosen to deliver the keynote address at the Corporation's annual Sales Conference to be held, because big American companies like to push out the boat on these occasions, in the Bahamas. English publishers stage these affairs in humbler venues like St Albans or in the case of Jonathan Cape, the publishers of this book, the Tower Hotel on the Embankment. Thither will be summoned, twice a year, Fred who represents the lists for London and Ireland; Antony for the South-east;

East Anglia is represented by Michael; David O. represents the West Country; Anne the West Midlands and Wales, David M. is in northern England; Andrew of course represents Scotland; Glyn the Australian M.D. is here, and Bob from Canada . . . These confrontations are the most important event in the life of a publishing house, for the publisher's sales team must be believed by the bookseller, if he or she is to succeed. A successful rep will be totally trusted by the bookseller who will also expect to be protected from over-ordering. 'Yes I know you did very well with the last Jeffrey Archer Mrs Prendergast, but this one isn't so good, half a dozen will be enough.' I am making this up, of course, but it is the sort of thing a good rep should say. Back to Jonathan Cape. In the plush ambience of the Tower Hotel, orchestrated by the Marketing Director, Roger, with Peter and Quentin, the Home and Export Directors, flanked by Rupert, Harriet and Linda from publicity, the team will be exhaustively enthused by the protagonists of the new titles they have to sell. On these occasions the Chairman (Tom Maschler) and the Managing Director (Graham C. Greene) will cast themselves more as advocates than Field-Commanders. It is a strange relationship because the reps have not participated to any serious extent in the selection of the merchandise they have to offer, although they may well be asked their opinion of a jacket or a project, or more commonly the right selling price.

The publishers' sales representatives are, like the booksellers they serve, a special breed, and they are generally well paid and well nourished because without their conscientious good performance the house cannot flourish. Often a sales force is such a heavy operation that smaller publishers cannot afford their own and must link up with one of the majors. The additional turnover generated by agenting other publishers' lists reduces the enormous overheads needed to employ anyone 'on the road' in the Western world today.

If Antony, Fred, Michael and co. can be enthused by the 'presentation' of a new title, so far so good, it remains only for the public to take the book out of the bookshop. The presentation of a lead title for which targets are set may be accompanied by the presence of the author and the managing director or chairman; the latter may suggest bonuses if targets are exceeded. If they remain po-faced all is not lost, because a good book will eventually find its own level, e.g. Rupert Sheldrake's *A New Science of Life* (q.v.).

This pre-publication internal warm-up is supported by trade advertising. Money spent on full-page ads in the *Bookseller* in London and *Publishers Weekly* (PW) in New York, is seldom wasted. The ads will contain promises of a publicity campaign, a promotional tour and invariably a mention of 'a major movie in the making'. Straight *solus* display ads in the literary pages of the posh papers impress authors and their agents but don't sell books. The Sunday *New York Times* Book Review might disprove this. A perfect publicity campaign has to be as well co-ordinated as an invasion. It can be very expensive, fraught and involve much loss of temper. Every publicity person has their own pet horror-story to tell of signing sessions where not one book is sold, authors drunk on the air, the hired Rolls-Royce sweeping up and the author doesn't get out.

Publishing is increasingly about publicity. When there is a new book every twenty minutes, the title which can grab the attention of the media by hook or by crook (though straightforward corruption is rare) wins. Publicity is more crucial in the USA where the market is bigger and more conformist. Jeffrey Archer tells how, at the beginning of a promotional tour for *Kane and Abel*, he had difficulty in getting space, air and exposure on the media, but he found no problem at the end because by then he had succeeded and become a bestselling author worthy of interviews, like a snake with its tail tucked into its mouth.

Marilyn Edwards, ex-publicity director of Jonathan Cape, says, 'Authors are very vulnerable; seeing a book being published is like seeing a baby being booted or kissed.' She adds, 'They all mind terribly about reviews whatever they say.' Ideally, the publication of a book should become a news story. A good strong review or, rather, good strong reviews across the board from the *TLS* to the *Sun* will pull sales. But if accompanied, or better, preceded, by news stories the sales will stick and grow. Nicholas Mosley's biography of his father caused great controversy, which was fermented by the Government's release of the 1940 state papers: newspapers ran articles on Sir Oswald for weeks. The public quarrel between Eisenhower and Montgomery did not damage the latter's memoirs. One of the cleverest pieces of publicity ever was for the book *Masquerade*, where the search for hidden treasure, to which the book was the clue, provoked Laker to organise trips for Americans to join in the hunt.

Routine book publicity would start with a serious – i.e. long – TV interview on the Russell Harty, Terry Wogan or South Bank Shows with Pebble Mill as a second string. (In the US, Johnny Carson or Dick Cavett interviews have great pull.) This will be succeeded by local TV and radio appearances throughout the country, press interviews interspersed by a steady stream of snippets in diary columns. Finally, the book should hit one or more of the bestseller lists: *Sunday Times* or *Bookseller* in the UK, *New York Times* and *Publishers Weekly* in the US. But there is no real way of keeping it there except through the phenomenon of actual sales stimulated by invincible and incorruptible word of mouth.

It is a relief for publishers to know that if the launch of a big book by a new writer really works, the operation does not need to be repeated with every subsequent offering. Harold Robbins can relax in the South of France around publication date, confidently sipping champagne.

It is often said that for a publisher the best author is a dead author (see 'lively' in the glossary). A recent bestseller was A. J. Cronin's *The Citadel*, due to a television series; satisfying sales are enjoyed with no effort from the publicity department for the same reasons by the publishers of Evelyn Waugh, John Galsworthy and Thomas Hardy. The writer must not be too dead, however. No copyright can be enjoyed from the reissue of Oscar Wilde and Conan Doyle because they have been dead for over fifty years.

The publicity director needs faith in the list, the endurance to be trampled on and the reassurance that he or she will not be long in the job.

A long, long time ago London publishers thought that a

title by a favourite author would benefit if introduced to the gentlemen of the press on publication day over a glass (or two or three) of sherry offered in the *piano nobile* of their Bloomsbury offices. But reviewers tended to leave their extra copy in a taxi, consoling themselves guiltily that it was too late anyway; the publishers' only dividend was often a snide paragraph in the Londoner's Diary. However, sherry is cheaper than hiring *The France* as Sol Stein did. Here is an example of a party that worked. Two rules were observed: one, the party was at least three weeks before publication and two, the book itself was not publicly displayed. Let me explain.

When the typescript of *A New Science of Life* by Rupert Sheldrake came to me, I dimly perceived that I was sailing in special waters and such was my excitement that one Sunday, a few days after its receipt and in the presence of our Managing Director, Antony White, we signed the contract. Rupert Sheldrake is no crank. The youngest fellow of Clare College, Cambridge, a Rosenheim Fellow of the Royal Society, a director of ICRISAT (crop research) in India, he *used* to be a regular guy, a member of the Establishment. I have known him irregularly for twenty years as an intelligent, modest and amusing fellow who could make anything scientific simple, at least in conversation. He once proved that homing pigeons operate through ESP rather than their sighting of the sun or any such mechanistic explanation, by kitting them out with cracked contact lenses. 'How', I asked, 'did they manage the last few hundred yards?' 'They walked,' he replied.

In *A New Science of Life* he looks at a more fundamental issue. Why does a cabbage seed, which under a microscope so resembles a cauliflower, grow up to be a cabbage? How does a dog which loses the use of a leg in an accident after a few weeks learn to run happily on three? Why is a cell in a human leg identical to that in an arm yet an arm is an arm and a leg is a leg?

There are no answers to these questions. The regular scientists maintain either that they will be discovered and we are on the way – witness DNA – or that growth is haphazard. Dr Rupert Sheldrake says that the direction for growth comes not from within the body, from the chemicals it contains, but from an outside force.

Dr Sheldrake suggests that the growth and development of living organisms is directed by 'morphogenetic fields across time and space'. He likens us (and crystals and fruit flies and worms) to television sets receiving signals from a transmitter. The signals direct or redirect an organism so that the motor mechanism of the wounded dog is physically readjusted to enable it to run on three legs, as if one's car grew another gear. They reform growing human cells from the experiences of past generations so that we can learn to ride bicycles more easily than our grandparents and our grandchildren will handle their computers as easily as a yoyo.

Those who believe in God will have no difficulty in identifying the source of these signals but this is a step which Dr Sheldrake meticulously refuses to take. Of course, it was this element which most excited me and which turned off the established scientific publishers.

It would be invidious here to list the names of the established houses known for their scientific lists who sometimes tenderly, sometimes roughly, but always at great length rejected this manuscript. No wonder they turned it down. It was as if a professor of medicine were to offer a book showing that mastectomy and open heart surgery were both dangerous and a waste of time and that the answer to most human ills, other than the obvious need to set broken limbs, was patience, kindness, comfort and prayer. What would happen to the medical editors and their authors? (Such a book has indeed been published in America and has, of course, been ignored.)

*A New Science of Life*, although it does not suggest that all scientific research is bunk, does imply that scientists in this particular field should abandon their test tubes and go back, not so much to the drawing board as to contemplation under, perhaps, an apple tree.

In the contract with the author, it was agreed that instead of an advance we should have a party. (Such arrangements do not endear one to literary agents.) There is some dispute among publishers, as I have mentioned, as to whether London parties are worthwhile but the effect of this one can be traced.

Two days later the *Time-Life* scientific correspondent, driving to his office, heard on the BBC Overseas Service a fifteen-minute interview with Rupert Sheldrake. He sent a cab to our office for a copy of the book, which was sent on Concorde, and telexed his office that this was not just a book – it was an event.

'A book for burning?' ran the headline in an editorial in *Nature*, a journal not known for losing its cool. It continued that Dr Sheldrake's book was an 'infuriating tract' and compared it to *Mein Kampf*. Why? People more qualified than I, Alex Comfort, Arthur Koestler, Brian Inglis, Lord Ashby and others, subsequently welcomed it as extraordinary. The *New Scientist* cracked a whip which sent the bandwagon rolling with an encouraging editorial as a flyer to a long review, and has frequently featured *A New Science of Life* in its correspondence columns ever since. Then followed, oh so slowly, the posh newspapers, including the *Guardian*, which obliged with an editorial. The bookselling trade, understandably enough – who would expect a scientific book from Blond & Briggs? – was slow to respond and the bulk of our orders were, and still are, from individuals all over the world.

Earlier I had submitted the typescript to an American publisher of independent status and mind without (I thought) a connection with the scientific world. He had shaken hands on a modest contract at the ABA in Atlanta and then he reneged. His partner and his most distinguished author had been incensed at his proposal to publish such 'codswallop'.

Despite this transatlantic reception before our own publication, we had printed 2,000 copies and published to a subscription of 171 copies. This was understandable. What did Blond & Briggs think it was doing with a slim volume by an unknown academic with a mildly pretentious but far from fizzy title at £12.50? In vain did our reps invoke the precedent of *Small is Beautiful* by E. F. Schumacher, published in 1973 with the same print number and the same relatively high price (which £3.25 was in those days).

Rupert was not disturbed – he had already pointed out that there existed another non-book-buying 'culture' of which publishers were not aware – scientists, engineers and technicians. Perhaps there is a lesson to be learnt here. Anyway, we soon reprinted and Paladin bought the paperback rights.

Jeremy Tarcher, whose firm is now a subsidiary of Houghton Mifflin, paid a bit more than his predecessor. An editor from perhaps the largest publisher in the world offered $40,000 for the reprint rights. That we have made money is satisfying, but perhaps even more so is the correspondence in *Nature*. Their editorial has been excoriated by professors from all over the world and Milton has been hurled at them at length twice. This quote from *Areopagitica* is surely heartening for us all: 'Who kills man kills a reasonable creature, God's image, but he who destroys a good book, kills reason itself.'

As a publisher I am ever alert for opportunities to push my wares. One morning I saw a comment at the top of *The Times* diary which said that there was a great reluctance to advertise on LWT during the showing of the American nuclear holocaust film *The Day After*. Just the spot to mention my new publication which is concerned with atomic problems, I thought, for surely several million people will be watching the programme. I immediately rang LWT, who were cautious, seeming nervous of controversy. They wanted to know exactly what I would be saying. 'Nothing,' I replied. 'I'd just like to show a picture of the book, in its jacket, in silence for ten seconds.'

'Silence is not allowed, it upsets the blind.'

'Well then, how about, "The facts you know: judge for yourself"?'

As no one else wanted to use advertising time, I had hoped to get the space for a song but, haggle as I might, it was sadly not to be. The media should really treat publishers with great regard, for so much of their material originates in book form.

A rich lady of my acquaintance once stared through the double-glazed windows of the Orangery bar of her overheated country house, as she cradled a vodkatini, and asked me, 'Anthony, why do we need birds, or for that matter, bees or insects, especially', as she swatted a fly, 'insects?' I attempted to explain that everything in nature had a point and a function and that insects were vital as pollinators.

Publishers have just that point and function, they are like bees behind a screaming headline or a smash television series or a box-office film success. They so often provide the germinal thought. This can be seen emerging from a discussion of the kind I have minuted at George Weidenfeld's project meeting (see Chapter III).

The importance of the role of the publisher is supremely recognized in France where, for instance, Gallimard got Jean Genet off his tax through one telephone call, and where the publisher's imprint often appears as a credit on a film. English publishers had enough muscle to retain retail price maintenance for books and to get books exempted from both Purchase Tax and VAT when these were introduced (although danger looms again), but they were not so good at seeing themselves acknowledged on film documentaries and newspaper features. Look in the very small print – often as tiny as this – and you will see what I mean.

The main story in every issue of a colour magazine or the back of the posh papers is invariably an extract or serialization from a book about to be published. The sales of these first serial rights are, for general or trade publishers, a big element in their net profit. For indeed, publishers of the kind listed in our main selection make little or no money on the sale of books and depend for their net profit on subsidiary rights of which sales to a newspaper are the most glamorous. A successful movie can be even more beneficial. Not simply because of the publisher's direct cut, which is often 10 per cent, but in the spin-off from the increased paperback sales. The publishers of *The Exorcist* barely covered their advance of £6,000 with a hardback sale of 8,000 copies at £2.25 in 1971, but a couple of years later *their* share (7 per cent) of a half-year royalty was £28,000. Film companies are always trying to bum free copies of new publications. The proper answer to such a request is to tell them to buy a copy at Hatchards, the cost of which will be deducted from their option money.

I know about *The Exorcist* because it was a book I turned down when it first came my way with a price of £3,000 on it. Six weeks later, in New York, after a talking to from Mark Jaffe, I bought it for £6,000 and made a small fortune. That was a bestseller I very nearly missed. Every publisher has stories of such nightmares, often told with boastful *Schadenfreude*. The publisher who never lands a bestseller in his career must be a poor, unloved, unlucky fellow but bestsellers are, by their very nature, freaks whose genius may not be immediately visible. The legends are endless. *Gone with the Wind* did the rounds before it found a home and Beatrix Potter had to marry a publisher before she found a lover for *Mrs Tiggywinkle*. Here are my stories of bestsellers with my reasons for saying no and how they came my way in the first place: *How to Live with Your Neurotic Dog* – the cover with a picture of a spaniel on a psychiatrist's couch was pinned up above my desk in 1957 before I started publishing. I got bored with it. See 'title fatigue'. *Valley of the Dolls* – I had just published *The Carpetbaggers* and was arrogant enough to imagine that I could do without that sort of thing. *In Praise of Older Women* – I like older women but not in that way. An interesting bunch, all told. *How to Live with Your Neurotic Dog* was a good title idea and there are books which have sold on this strength alone, but after a while title fatigue sets in and they are just depressing. Long titles which have sold mediocre books include *Bury My Heart at Wounded Knee* and *By Grand Central Station I Sat Down and Wept*. Such length takes up a great deal of jacket space so does not stand out in a book window display nor on the spine: it does however trip off the tongue well and intrigue. There is a recognition factor in titles: many people mixed Nancy Milford with Nancy Mitford and when Lord David Cecil published his biography of Melbourne entitled *Lord M* in the 1950s, it was bought by people who thought it concerned Lord Montagu of Beaulieu.

Today many books are not only promoted and publicized in the usual ways, they are also packaged and merchandized. I have already mentioned *The Country Diary of an Edwardian Lady* as an example of a packaged book in Chapter VII. Michael Joseph published Rowena Stott's great aunt Edith Holden's diary, which has sold more than 2·5 million copies in hardback alone, in 1977 and subsequently sold the merchandizing rights to Nigel French and Pauline Deppé, who would get approximately 5 to 10 per cent profit from everything sold with Edith Holden's drawings and paintings decorating it, whether a postcard or a teacup. In the case of the illustrated *Lark Rise to Candleford*, a merchandizing company has been set up which will exploit the book in every media commercially, retaining 50 per cent of such merchandizing royalties, whilst Oxford University Press (the original hardback publishers), Anthony Cheetham of Century (the buyers of the illustrated abridged rights), and Shuckburgh Reynolds (the packagers), split 50 per cent. The merchandizers have sub-licensed furniture makers, jam and preserve producers, clothing firms and other manufacturers to tie in with Flora Thompson's Victorian world.

Perhaps the classic example of merchandizing was the *Preppy Handbook* in America where Peter and Carolan of Workman Publications in New York sold preppy T-shirts, diaries, tennis racquets, the lot. In England the *Sloane Ranger's Handbook* might well prove a good candidate for this sort of promotion. More usual is a book in the children's market: the Mr Men books ended up as flavours of yoghurt. A new candidate is SuperTed, a Welsh bear which began life on S4C, the Welsh language commercial channel. SuperTed was in a 50p booklet published by Frederick Muller, then appeared on BBC1, where his audience climbed from 1·9 to 3·4 million in six weeks, has been taken up by Walt Disney and the National Coal Board's pension fund, is bringing employment to Cardiff and can now be seen on lollipops and shoes, bubble-bath bottles, slippers, jigsaws and tote bags.

The chain stores, notably Marks & Spencer, have recently seen that they can sell more books than bookshops, more liquor than liquorshops and more fish than fishmongers. M. & S. are now the biggest fishmongers in England and sell more than £12 million worth of books a year. The line is selected just like a bra, pre-tested, with every element precisely specified from a few select suppliers such as Paul Hamlyn, David Frost (Paradine Productions) or George Weidenfeld. The initial print order of 50,000-plus enables them to give, as with other products, good value for money in a limited, and I would say, somewhat boring range.

Marks & Spencer asked Caroline Conran to write their

book on English cooking; now her husband Terence Conran is about to enter the same area of publishing in conjunction with Octopus and their product will be sold in Mothercare – under the imprint Mothercon? In fact Sir Terence and Paul Hamlyn are now joined in 'Conran Octopus', shipping coffee-table books to the US in *containers*!

Selling and promoting books is tough and idiosyncratic: straight advertising in the posh papers appeals to author and agent and publicity can be a two-way horror. However, even trouble sells books . . . I began this chapter by mentioning John Menzies, the biggest booksellers and wholesalers in Scotland. Well, their board bothered to ban *101 Uses for the Unemployed* by Neuman and Neuman, a small £1.95 paperback book of cartoons. The ban was remarked upon by *The Times* in its gossip column and the book's sales increased.

## *Remainders*

It is impossible to print the perfect number of any book: it's always either too few or too many, mostly too many. What happens to them? If sales don't occur, then the useless stock may have to be pulped or remaindered. The late Walter Harrap, apart from saying, 'Let's take a risk and turn it down,' was also fond of the adage that no publisher ever goes bust from the books he doesn't print. But optimism, the (false) exigencies of costing and the knowledge that every book has some value makes for over-printing. Enter the remainder merchant who, despite his funereal role, is a cheerful, ebullient fellow with a ready chequebook – sometimes even ready cash – a tendency to smoke cigars and not remove his over-coat (they also give the booziest parties in the trade). They have access to outlets publishers know not of, and do not wish to know, from Tasmania to department stores in Lew-isham. The millionaire Paul Hamlyn started this way with a barrow. Most publishers in permanent negative cash-flow situations are only too delighted to deal with them. However, it is wise when remaindering the works of a grand and touchy man of letters to beseech the remainder merchant only to market what he has bought in Australia – unless it is by Patrick White.

When contemplating the production of an expensive art book, a nervous publisher may guarantee the remainder merchant a fixed price *before* the book is even printed, let alone sold; this is called a 'put'. It's a longstop in case all goes awry. It means that a proportion of the print run is picked up at a lower than guaranteed price. If the publisher sells out his own edition at full price, all well and good and the deal is off. The same arrangement might be repeated over a reprint. Nowadays books are remaindered very quickly to save money on warehousing and overheads, sometimes, it seems, before the public are ready, which puts the secondhand value of the book right up.

When I was last in America I went to see Bruce Harris, who has worked for the last twenty-one years for the totally independent publishing house of Crown, owned by one eighty-year-old man, Nat Wartels. Bruce started in the firm by selling remainders.

> I would get 2,000 of a wonderful book, sell them and not have any more. But as a book person I realized it was not intelligent to run out of your best book, which is of course the inherent difficulty in remaindering, so I thought there must be a better way. Therefore I made a new kind of contract in which I bought the publishing rights in remaindered books for a minimal sum and a royalty and reprinted them as paperbacks. In that sense I guess I was manufacturing our remainders, taking copies of books which were sitting around moribund and selling them off. I try to be creative. If I see that we are selling a lot of remaindered books on railroads, then I say we must have our own books on railroads. We have 20,000 active titles between all the Crown companies now.
>
> If I really like a book there is a chance it will make money, for it is safe to say that 10,000 other crazy people can be found somewhere who will like it too. That is why I am in the position I am in.

In a way Hamlyn and Octopus over here both also manufacture remainders for they have remainder prices on their original publications which they have printed 100,000 of in the beginning.

I have never heard a little boy say that he wanted to be a remainder merchant when he grew up but it is a perfectly honourable profession.

# XI *Bookshops*

King's Lynn in the days of cutback and caution isn't perhaps the happiest place to own your own bookshop but John Prime and his wife Maureen had faith: they had just moved to a brand-new site, slap in the middle of a spanking new shopping precinct when I visited them. We traipsed past Littlewoods, Marks & Spencer, Etam, 'the utilities' and W. H. Smith, deeper and deeper into one of the largest planned complexes I'd seen until we came to the Prime Bookshop. Modern, shiny, paperbacked, with yards of invitingly displayed categories and very, very few hardbacks. Upstairs, and the stairs are luckily situated at the back of the shop, is his new and successful bargain book section. (People have to pass the real books to get there and you never know . . .) John Prime is probably quite right to be in the centre of a shopping mall – anyone can buy books, not only the cultured folk you might expect, the *TLS* and Sunday review readers (they are often the very worst when it comes to actually forking out – they use libraries and wait for birthdays and Christmas).

Talking of clientele, John Prime had the most charming story, which tells much about the place he serves. Norfolk has no real 'middle class', as he put it. There are royals galore – Sandringham is not far away and the sister of the Princess of Wales often drops in; there is the 'Tec, but not a rich one', farmers who have tremendous ups and downs and the fishermen and canners whose tenure is extremely dicey, and especially bad at the moment. But it's the poor who come in and want a proper book (hardback) for their money, as a book is a sacred, useful, enjoyable thing to own. Gypsies are great customers and constantly ask Mr Prime's advice as to the best book for their children. Other parents are not too good in this area. The royals, however, go for easy reads and always in paperback. They are enchanted when a present can cost as little as £1.50.

Staple dictionaries go well; people want the ones they know, like OUP or Collins with Cassell's for German and Harrap's for French. What is actually sold is pretty predictable and people conventional with the odd whim. For example, mothers and teachers go for all the pocket Observer books and Puffins. Racier, unfamiliar children's books, lovely though they may be, aren't safe bets to stock. Cooking and gardening sell for ever? Yes, but . . . it depends a lot on the season, Christmas being the best as it's present-buying time, the books with a wealth of colour illustrations selling in hardback and the classics in paperback. Michel Guérard's *Cuisine Minceur* and *Nouvelle*, which is a new phenomenon, didn't do well in hardback, but sold lots in paperback. The answer there is that cooking and gardening are not such safe publishing bets. Guidebooks and Teach Yourself sell if they are cheap (it seems the contents don't really bother the user – rather surprising if one compares the cost of a book to that of a holiday). Berlitz guides go very well, and out of the expensive guides *Guide Bleu* is most popular. Ordnance Survey maps are consistent sellers. Romance and fishing are fine. Thrillers keep the recession out but people are not adventurous and, as John Prime put it, 'are just catching up with P. D. James'.

Royalty and money are excellent recession books, however mediocre, and the Royal Wedding went on selling up to Christmas and after, even the bad colour 'Colour Library' quickie. Jeffrey Archer has really found his métier and makes everyone extremely happy. In fact John Prime thinks the *Sunday Times* list is the very best guide to bestsellers although 'a lot of people will contradict me on this'. Two charming and unexpected little facts did emerge during our discussion of yawn, yawn, what sells. Antiques are out and poetry is in. No doubt those who used to love antiqueing every Saturday no longer have the money, so a book on the subject would make them terribly unhappy, whereas a slim vol. of Penguin poetry will go on for eternity and keep them at home, contemplating.

The sad fact is that John Prime just can't afford to stock many hardbacks, especially fiction (this makes all hardback publishers sad too but they just have to understand) and good old – and new – Penguin is still the overall saviour. All Virago books sell well and John Prime puts this down (partly) to 'their very distinctive appearance'.

John Prime is a jolly fellow and knows, after thirteen years on his own, that the book trade isn't the easiest one to be in so he does quite a few publicity stunts, which work. Forget the boring midday signing session. Mr Prime's secret is a drink in the evening in the shop with the author who will, of course, sign his books. Sometimes he gives a dinner, as he did for Richard Adams on the publication of *Shardik*, but this was preceded by a children's signing in the afternoon, a television interview plus three local radio outfits in the shop and the papers. Everyone rolled up and naturally the very sight of the shop and Mr Adams on television did the Prime bookshop no harm at all. John Prime sweetly conceded that he was frightened that Richard Adams was going to live up to his (falsely) reported reputation and turn out to be 'a conceited old bugger' – in the event he was charming and most obliging. When, at the end of dinner John Prime asked Mr Adams why he was being so pleasant he replied, 'I've just been offered $300,000 for my hard and paper American rights. THAT'S WHY.'

Edward Heath came to a signing party at the shop and they sold (an extra?) 150 copies at £5.95 of his sailing book. King's Lynn is a bit out of the way so how does he manage to lure big names to the mall? 'Nag them.'

So much for the public, the Prime publicity wheezes, but who are his 'bête noires'? The reps who don't have the authority to take back unsold copies. Returns are a nightmare and the publisher often as not doesn't want to know. Writing to a sales manager and pleading for mercy is all too often like getting blood out of a stone, so why does he bother to deal with such stubborn people? Because of the reps themselves? 'They use a hell of a lot of petrol. Some come twice and some four times a year. Some are absolutely useless. I get about ten a week.' To give some idea of the levels of rep life and intelligence Mr Prime divulged that – the Thames & Hudson rep is pretty well informed, not an art lover but has done his homework and will know if there's a tie-in. The Gollancz rep comes on the Nottingham run and will be through in ten minutes. Neither of these will take returns. Rocky Stone from Pan has a nose and makes one listen but Prime's favourite – an old friend from Manchester days possessing both authority and knowledge – is Eddie Hutchfield. With that we decided to go to lunch on the first day of a first-time entry to *The Good Food Guide* overlooking the brown oozie Ouse, where we prayed for the day of the powerful rep with muscle who would solve problems, proffer advice and save endless time, confusion and anguish.

John Prime's problems are those of so many bookshops: few customers for much of the year, too many of whom want only one cheap paperback or a single copy of something he doesn't have in stock. Too many browsers, too much stock. It's so hard for a bookseller to get rid of titles which are cluttering up his shelf space because they turned out to be unpopular. He may sell them off at a discount during National Book Sale week but if the locals didn't care for them in the first place, when they were new and all the rage, they probably won't want them when they are soiled and jaded. It would be a good idea if bookshops swopped dud stock with a shop in another area during National Book Sale week, for such a move would bring cut-price, different titles to a new public.

John Prime seemed to be keeping well afloat when I saw him but within a few months he had had to close down. Was he too far away from London, too remote? Did those living in more prosperous, more heavily populated areas do better, have different problems? To find out I went to see The Bookshop, Virginia Water.

In the neck of the woods where the Rolls-Royce and the

Volkswagen Golf are the common form of transport, it is not surprising to find a bookshop in which a customer may pick up sixty pounds' worth of new novels in a morning. What is surprising perhaps, is that the owners should be Bryan Forbes, actor, director, writer and his wife Nanette Newman, also a writer, whose children's books sell half a million copies a year. The fruits of their literary activity are evident in the little shop ('all too', said Frank Muir who was there when I visited), but otherwise it is a regular, efficient Charter bookshop, that is, one which guarantees to obtain books which customers ask for, to carry essential trade reference books, such as Whitaker's *Books in Print*, to train its assistants, to send them on special courses and to maintain various basic standards, in return for which it should get better trade terms from publishers (not all comply). Bryan Forbes's bookshop turns over its stock of £40,000 twice a year yielding enough profit to maintain a manager at £10,000 a year. Not that Bryan Forbes isn't an active bookseller himself; he sees publishers' sales representatives, tots up, wraps up, and writes indignant letters to the *Bookseller*. He also holds strong views, especially on book clubs.

Before going on to hear these, however, it is necessary to digress for one moment to explain that all *bona fide* bookshops support the Net Book Agreement which binds them to retail price maintenance, that is to sell the books at the price printed on the jacket and not to cut this, however much they are tempted. If a book has been on their shelves for over a year, they may try to sell it off during National Book Sale week at a discount, but they may only do this during that one week. The Net Book Agreement was invented to help booksellers, to encourage them to stock a wide range of titles, knowing that the shop down the road, which might be larger, could not undercut them at a whim; it was upheld when retail price maintenance on other goods declined in the hope that booksellers would flourish all over the country, not just in university towns, so that children and other interested parties could broaden their minds by finding and buying interesting literature, both educational and otherwise. It was feared that if bookshops could undercut each other at random, few would be left except those purveying comics and pornography. However, as Bryan Forbes points out, book clubs undercut bookshops with impunity.

> Not so long ago I fired off a letter to the *Bookseller* on this very subject as I was incensed that current bestsellers were being offered, through national advertising, at flea-market prices. This, I feel, makes nonsense of the Net Book Agreement and is, in fact, very short-sighted. The original conception of book clubs was an excellent one which was of benefit to both publisher and author and did not cut across the efforts of the average bookseller who struggles to make a modest living. The special book club editions were seldom produced until a year after the original hardback publication and they actually appeared in a different format. Undoubtedly, they spread the word and encouraged people who seldom, if ever, entered a bookshop, to sample the delights of literature. Alas, this concept has gone by the board and now there seems to be a concentrated and determined effort to slip through the Net Book Agreement by the back door by the simple use of muscle. I deplore this and I am convinced that, sooner or later, booksellers will rise up and take to the barricades – and I might well lead them. The situation has to be made more equitable because I cannot, without fear of penalty, reduce the price of current books, and yet others, with impunity, can it seems.

Bryan Forbes was kinder about publishers but then it depended which hat he was wearing.

> Casting aside my bookseller's cap and replacing it with my author's chapeau, my favourite publisher is the one I am with at the moment, Michael Joseph, and long may it continue to be so. My least favourite publisher is a particularly arrogant American pedant who recently sent me a rejection slip of such startling nastiness that I immediately sat down at my IBM Displaywriter and fired off a literary exocet missile that I hope will sink him for good. Publishing used to be an occupation for gentlemen, I am told, but

nowadays it seems to be a kindergarten for failed writers who labour under the impression that they are budding Prousts. Switching hats yet again, I find that, as a bookseller, the efficiency of publishers seems to coincide with the cycles of the moon – one year they get the computer right and books arrive on time and in good condition, but before one can sit back and view the situation with any complacency, they go to the bottom of the league and somebody else takes over. The most spectacular disaster I have experienced was when a paperback house sent me thirty dumpbins instead of three single-order copies. It was literally impossible to move in the shop and my anguished telephone call to their sales department seemed to fall on indifferent ears. It was only my threat to throw the entire lot into the street that produced any results.

As a general rule, most of the display material is extremely rickety (dumpbins, for instance, seem to self-destruct the moment one unpacks them and they are a continuing hazard to customers). Shop space is usually at a premium and if I accepted every piece of display material offered, my own shop would soon resemble a jumble sale. I think the intentions are always good, but the execution is generally second-rate.

As a film director, I have always tried to treat my extras as human beings and not as cattle, and I have tried to apply the same attitude towards publishers' reps. I think they have an extremely difficult task to perform, are often not fully supported by the publishers themselves, in that they are often sent out into the wilderness unarmed – lacking proof copies and adequate display material. There is no trick to selling copper-bottomed bestsellers, but the average book needs a great deal of advance publicity in order that the bookseller can make a proper evaluation. I think I can say that both myself and my manager, Patric Glasheen, always try to welcome reps, give them a cup of tea, and fan their fevered brows with old copies of Whitaker's. To elaborate on what I mean by sending them out unarmed, it would help enormously if they were trusted more and given the authority to make on-the-spot decisions regarding returns. This would save a lot of unnecessary paperwork and enable booksellers to balance the amount of returns against future orders, thus increasing turnover. To have to wait up to three months for an authorization for returns is both unfair and ridiculous. Without any criticism of the reps themselves, if I find a publisher who is extremely tardy with returns, I send the rep away empty-handed and order through my wholesaler. I think this is to be regretted but it is forced on me on certain occasions.

My other hobby-horse is that I am convinced that, during the all-important Christmas period, all reps should travel with very large car stocks. I cannot understand why more publishers don't employ this method because at Christmas most of the buying is impulse buying and if a book goes out of stock, that sale is lost for ever, to the detriment of all concerned. But, long live the reps, whom I greatly respect.

By the end of the harangue, I felt that poor Bryan must be fed up with books, particularly those slow-moving hardback novels, but no, he is a passionate supporter of hardback fiction which he feels is 'the seed corn of the future'. He cheerfully admitted that he had never lost his love of books, 'although I readily appreciate the growth of the paperback market and welcome it, there is nothing, in my mind, as exciting as a freshly printed hardback edition that one settles down with to enjoy and which later graces our shelves. I may be a purist, but the same thrill is not forthcoming from a paperback edition, however well printed.'

Bookshops today are having a hard time: there are few left who just sell books, most eke out their turnover with stationery, magazines, posters, calendars, bits and bobs. Even W. H. Smith some years ago seemed to be selling more fancy goods than books, but of late, they have increased the range they stock and now even offer to take single-copy orders. I'm a W. H. Smith fan for when I had a walk-out with Sarah Miles she introduced me to David Benedictus and I published his novel about Eton, *The Fourth of June*. Naturally I expected the Eton bookshop to take a great many copies but they absolutely refused, whereas the Windsor branch of W. H. Smith sold five hundred in a 'half'.

The single-copy order has always been the bane of all bookshops but electronics may at last be coming to the rescue. Austick of Leeds now offer a twenty-four-hour service and advertise their telephone number widely – 0532 432446. I dialled and left my request and my credit card number with their answering service. Three days later I received their catalogue and a pleasant note to say that unfortunately the two books I had asked for were out of stock. Presumably, had they been in stock, I would have received them with the catalogue, that is within three days. An excellent new system which really does work.

The Book Token service has also improved, for since 1967 there has been no time limit. The shop selling the token retains 12½ per cent of its value, which is not as much as if the shop had sold a book but the token has taken up no space, demanded no capital. The service is used by 300,000-odd customers a year so could also be said to be a success.

Booksellers are a dedicated breed, sober, cautious and impossible to excite (their assistants tend to be mousy and underpaid); a few are rude and interesting like Ian Norrie of High Hill Bookshop, Hampstead, whose letters to the trade press would make a plangent volume. Britain, however, is lucky to be endowed with many famous family firms who soldier on, Austick's of Leeds, Smith's of Glasgow, Bauermeister's of Edinburgh and Heffer's of Cambridge, but the crown must go to Blackwell's of Oxford. Their current title file is based on Whitaker's *British Books in Print* but it is more up-to-date, since it combines the cataloguing information from the national libraries with the commercial information from their own dealings with publishers. This amazing list forms the basis for their new English books service standing-order system. All is computerized.

# XII *Libraries*

Fifty-one per cent of the population – over 28 million people – visited a public library in 1982, which is higher than the attendance at museums, pop concerts, cinemas and even football games, according to a MORI survey. It is less surprising a figure when one remembers that libraries in Great Britain are free and warm, unlike New York where the public libraries seem mostly to be closed. Furthermore it is estimated that 649 million loans are made each year from British libraries.

Britain has a unique library system. Everyone in the country can borrow almost any book for nothing. This noble Victorian concept is often literally engraved on the red-glazed portals of the portentous and homely buildings in the industrial north. Librarians find offensive the notion that the reading public should have to pay for their pleasures as they do for swimming baths and public lavatories, which are also maintained by the ratepayer. The only people who suffer from this free loan of over 500 million books a year are the authors and publishers. Public libraries are administered by local authorities who vary in their generosity, roughly, according to their political hue. Most councils are philistine and examine the number rather than the quality of the 'issues' when deciding how much public money to allocate. In times of recession, ironically when more people have more time on their hands, culture is the first to be cut, although in 1982 the Minister for the Arts was successful in persuading a Conservative government that the opposite should be done. (In ancient Athens performances of Euripides and Aeschylus were commonly paid for by mine-owners.)

Local authorities put out contracts to library suppliers and a few firms, like Askew's of Preston, Holt Jackson of St Anne's and Brown's of Hull, supply most of England, irrespective of geography. They order, like booksellers, from jackets, and the more intelligent librarians from reviews in *The Times Literary Supplement*. Their orders account for at least 10 to 15 per cent of a publisher's print run, although houses like Robert Hale and Mills & Boon depend much more on library sales than some others. Certain fiction known to sell well to libraries may be sold in sheet-form by the publisher to a library contractor, who then has the sheets specially bound in very tough, durable material.

Dr Peter Mann, a sociologist who has studied the behaviour of borrowers in public libraries, says that adult fiction accounts for over 60 per cent of books issued: mysteries are the most popular, followed by romances, historical novels and adventure in that order. Another study by Nicholas Spenceley suggested that those who took out a book without knowing anything about it, or its author, beforehand, were often disappointed, whereas if they had reserved the book, or had heard of the author, they were much more likely to have enjoyed and appreciated what they had read.

Clearly, therefore, there is a great need to make borrowers more aware of who is who in libraries in order to make them enjoy their reading more. Dr Mann also feels strongly that more should be done to help borrowers move on to new authors by telling them about authors similar to the one whose book they have just read. All too often, if they find their favourite author's works are all out on loan, or if they have read them all, they just grab the nearest brightly coloured book off the shelf, which leads to dissatisfaction. What is needed is either a helpful librarian or a list hung on the wall which makes suggestions, saying if you liked A's works, then you might also enjoy B's. If you are crazy about the sea, how about trying C. S. Forester or Richard Hough: a browser's catalogue in fact. It would make a good party game: name six authors similar to Catherine Cookson or Louis D'Amour. Who would you team alongside Iris Murdoch out of the following: Phyllis Bentley, Arthur Hailey, Jean Plaidy or Leslie Thomas? It also lends itself to fascinating diagrams where those who write detective stories and romantic fiction, like Georgette Heyer, can be made to form links between Raymond Chandler and Barbara Cartland or Dick Francis and Anya Seaton. In the same way Graham Greene and John Le Carré can be linked to cookery writers through Len Deighton and so on . . .

Philip Larkin gives a dry, perspicacious account of what it was like to be a librarian in the 1940s in *Early Days at Leicester*: 'understaffed, underequipped, underfinanced, they battled on through the lean years, reckoning no task beneath them: the sheer numbers of books they ordered, accessioned, catalogued, classified, issued, kept track of, sent for binding and all the rest of it would make – does make – a latter-day chief Librarian blench.' For today all is being – or is about to be – computerized in the library world. Many libraries are now linked nationally and internationally into a vast bibliographic network including the British Library and the British National Bibliography and with trade bibliographies such as Whitaker's and Blackwell's. If a title isn't recorded on one of these computers, however, it is completely lost. Maybe it will soon be possible to order library books through Prestel.

Incidentally, the Australian National Library is linked to Washington Library's network for a main source of information on English language books. Australian libraries are therefore likely to order the American edition of any title rather than the United Kingdom one unless the British get their book titles down on the Washington computer.

To find out more about libraries and librarians, I asked around and sent out a questionnaire. There was, I discovered, a great interest in making local libraries into places for meetings and talks, film shows, exhibitions and places where children could play and be read stories in order to encourage more local citizens to see their libraries as cheerful community centres. Cold culture inhibits. Too often libraries are seen as back-up centres for adult education programmes and local authority evening classes, not as places where the unemployed can come to relax and find pleasure.

I was delighted to hear one librarian say that he thought books should be sold in libraries either in a 'shop' run by the local bookseller or on a commission basis. After all, nothing can be more frustrating than finding the book you want is already out on loan, or that the latest Dick Francis hasn't yet been catalogued: to be able to buy a copy then and there would be a bonus for all. Others thought that libraries were under-used and that more market research could be done to find out what borrowers would like; many thought more periodicals should be left lying around to make the atmosphere more casual and cheerful. Perhaps a greater aura of fun should be exuded by libraries and less noble-mindedness.

As well as the ordinary local public libraries in Great Britain, there are six privileged libraries who must, by statute, be sent a copy of every book published: they are the British Library, the National Libraries of Scotland and of Wales, the Bodleian, Cambridge University Library, and the library of Trinity College Dublin. Giving a copy to the London Library is an elegant option. The late Mark Longman felt passionately about giving away these six books and talked about going to gaol rather than submitting. But he never did. It should rather be regarded as a fine on immortality. What do these ancient places do with all those tons of free books sent to them? More have been published in the last thirty years than in the history of mankind: no wonder the British Library tried to knock down streets of Holborn for their accommodation.

In 1979 the Public Lending Right became law, after a long campaign led by Brigid Brophy, Maureen Duffy, Victor Bonham Carter and others. Under this Act authors were to receive some benefit when their books were taken out (and read?) from public libraries. The Government set aside £2 million in 1984 for this, of which £376,000 went to organize the initial pilot scheme whereby computer recordings were made in sixteen sample libraries during six months of 1983 in order to assess the snags; £36,000 went to local authorities and just over £1½ million to the authors. Many people feared that most of the cash would go to a few hardy perennials who were already millionaires with tax problems, thus leaving little for struggling young novices. To counteract this a maximum was set at £5,000 and a minimum at £1. At a penny a library book borrowed, no one looks like making a fortune, although Jeffrey Archer hit the maximum and Barbara Cartland did very well, appealing to 415,359 readers with her 242 titles, which netted her a handsome £4,984. But the joy is not all in the money, the recognition factor is a great morale booster. Tim Jeal was delighted to receive a computer print-out telling him that a cheque for £500 would soon be on its way from the PLR fund: he rang his agent, overjoyed. The psychological stimulation of knowing that your books have been read by thousands of people is great. Jeal's hardback novel *A Marriage of Convenience* had been taken out 23,618 times and his biography of Livingstone, published in 1974, had been loaned to 7,000 people. Not only do such figures hearten the writer, they also provide ammunition for agents making future negotiations with publishers and paperback houses.

Many writers failed to fill in the forms or to have each of their titles witnessed by a solicitor at £2 a time, others live abroad, but over 6,000 received something. There were 81 authors in the Jeffrey Archer/Barbara Cartland class; 247 receiving, with Brian Aldiss, between £1,000 and £3,000; 317 along with Noel Barber, whose *Tanamera*, set in Singapore, brought him £878; 1,516 authors got between £100 and £500, whilst the largest number of all, 3,878, received less than £100. Undoubtedly more people will fill the forms in correctly next year.

Barbara Cartland's cheque is a reflection of, and on, the taste of England. As long as the success, and funding, of the public libraries depends on the number of titles issued, it cannot claim to be a sincere patron of the arts.

# XIII *Prizes*

Twelve bottles of claret, malt whisky, an engraved goblet, a brass carriage clock, a magnifying glass, £10, £10,000 or something in between, are offered as prizes, some annually, to those engaged in the book world whether it be as librarians, indexers, bibliographers, cartoonists, prose or poetry writers, automotive journalists or translators. To be eligible for one of 140-odd awards, you may have written an unpublished essay on Scottish history within the reigns of James I and James VI not exceeding 10,000 words; have added to folklore; have researched in the Marxist tradition of Isaac Deutscher, have contributed more than anyone else that year to the civilized appreciation of food and drink, live in Greenwich or Wandsworth, be under forty-one or a teenager. You may have increased the world's understanding of the freedom of the individual in society, like the Cobden Trust Award, worth £100, or changed the world's understanding (period) like the Nobel Prize, worth £80,000.

A detailed guide to these prizes, awards and grants is published by the National Book League and can be obtained from 45 East Hill, London SW18. The 1982 edition omits two of the richest United Kingdom prizes altogether: The Wolfson Literary Award for history and biography, now in its eleventh year and worth £15,000, and the Betty Trask Award of £12,500 for the first romantic or traditional novel written by someone under thirty-five, in its first year. Miss

Trask left £400,000 when she died in January 1983, aged eighty-eight, and was the author of *Love has Wings*, *I Tell my Heart* and *Love has no Limits*, all published by William Collins, plus fifty more. The richest of all is, of course, the Nobel Prize for Literature, won in 1983 by William Golding, whose publisher is Faber & Faber.

But there is no need for a writer to wait until old age to receive recognition in this country, there are many awards worth a respectable thousand pounds or so and well worth having. There is the James Tait Black Memorial Prize, which always looks good when printed on a jacket; there is a prize given by the Angel Hotel, Bury St Edmunds, another by Collins for a contribution to the relevance of Christianity in the modern world and there is also one worth £2,000 given in memory of Georgette Heyer for an outstanding historical novel. There are even six worth £1,000 each given to those making the most outstanding contribution to motorcycling.

Three superb new arrivals on the scene are the £5,000 Sinclair prize for fiction, Sotheby's International poetry competition on behalf of the Arvon foundation, also worth £5,000, and the Mitchell Prize for an outstanding contribution to art history worth $10,000.

Some are very modest, hardly enough to support a celebratory sherry party, others encourage travel or further research, but all help to stimulate an interest in books, give a sense of recognition and achievement to writers and – in the case of the best known prize of all, the Booker – actually increase sales.

Why is the Booker such a success when even grander prizes in America and France carry so little clout? It's not just the money, the £15,000 to the winner, nor is it the influence of the donors. It has become a media event. It has, in the words of Martyn Goff, director of the National Book League, 'consistently provided a news quotient that builds up year after year'. Because the Booker Prize is newsworthy, winning it can transform an author's commercial future. Even being a runner-up makes a huge difference to sales.

The Booker Prize was set up in 1968 by Booker McConnell, an industrial conglomerate primarily dabbling in sugar, whose literary connections were through copyright ownership of Ian Fleming and Agatha Christie. It has brought them public recognition on a scale rare for a trading company. The original money offered to reward merit was £5,000 but in 1976 this amount was doubled. Scandal boosted publicity early on. When John Berger received the award for his novel *G*, he announced at the prize dinner that he was giving half his cheque to the Black Panther movement. Then the following year Lord Butler raised many hackles when presenting the cheque to J. G. Farrell for *The Siege of Krishnapur* by making some dubious joke which hit the headlines. By 1980 the press was all agog when two literary giants, Anthony Burgess and William Golding, fought for the honour. That year the wily Peter Mayer of Penguin Books bought the paperback rights to five out of the six short-listed books and published all five a fortnight before the final decision was made so that the public could judge for themselves. When Golding won with *Rites of Passage* it went on to sell 56,000 copies in hardcover. The runner-up, Burgess's *Earthly Powers*, did well too, selling over 40,000.

Slowly the prestige and excitement engendered by the whole brouhaha has mounted. In 1981, Salman Rushdie's *Midnight's Children* pipped all at the post, turning a first printing of 2,500 copies into a runaway 20,000 within six months. The runner-up, D. M. Thomas's *The White Hotel*, also gained a sales leap from all the press mentions, trade copies went up by 16,000 and a book club took 8,500.

But one of the grandest coups of all time was the fourteenth winner, *Schindler's Ark*, and, thanks to Ion Trewin of Hodder & Stoughton, here's how the Booker catapulted Thomas Keneally into the big league.

By 1982, people were becoming conscious that the Booker was good, newsworthy stuff and the press were alert for controversy. They got it right away with *Schindler's Ark* for as soon as the book was short-listed there was an outcry suggesting that it was not really a work of fiction. The debate was fierce. It grew fiercer on television. With great self-control no one on the committee had breathed the winner's name until the glare of the television lights focused on the chairman

Some three million people were said to have watched the announcement at a dinner in the City of London.

Within hours booksellers besieged Hodder & Stoughton, standing on the doorstep, pushing and shoving to get in. The first day's orders were for 7,000 copies. To make distribution fair a special computer program was devised: if a bookshop had originally ordered 100 and now wanted to reorder 1,000 and there were, say, only 2,000 in the warehouse, then the bookshop would end up with 634 as its fair share. This was an attempt to encourage those bookshops which had backed their own original judgment initially with a large order: after all, they had stuck their necks out with their first response; such loyalty should be acknowledged.

The first printing of Thomas Keneally's *Schindler's Ark* to the trade and book club market had been 17,500 copies of which subscriptions up to October 15th, 1982 had been 4,449. The Booker Prize was awarded on October 19th:

| | | |
|---|---|---|
| October | 22 | 7,475 |
| | 29 | 17,068 |
| November | 6 | 17,445 |
| | 12 | 24,986 |
| | 19 | 27,736 |
| | 26 | 31,776 |
| December | 3 | 33,113 |
| | 10 | 34,525 |
| | 17 | 38,020 |
| | 23 | 39,375 |
| January | 31 | 40,011 |
| April | 30 | 41,250 |

By the end of 1982 Australian sales had reached 21,000 and book club sales 34,000. By the end of 1983, book club sales had reached 103,000 and Coronet UK paperback sales were over 300,000. But sales did not end there, word of mouth has publicized the story far and wide; the book seems to have touched an essential chord in some people, it has even been used as text for sermons; the theme appears to have immense appeal and the sales have continued to mount, without any signs of flagging, ever since.

But that is not all. Several of Keneally's earlier works were successfully reissued in hardback and paperback, though whether future sales of Keneally's books will always now be in the super-league remains uncertain. They may do well if he sticks to the same kind of book but if he writes an entirely different oeuvre, say a light modern novel, then he may not carry his public with him. It will be interesting to see if Keneally can prove himself a second time round. Once he has done that, then no doubt he can afford to be more experimental.

That some people thought the Booker Prize-winning magic was not for always was brought home by a scathing comment in the *Sunday Times* by Leslie Geddes Brown on the poor sales of the 1983 winner, *The Life and Times of Michael K* by J. M. Coetzee. However, Secker & Warburg, the publishers, pointed out that as far as they were concerned the sales were pretty impressive: the book sold 5,910 copies before the short-list was drawn up, and another 5,002 copies before the winner was known. After the prize was announced it sold 23,015 to bookshops (although how many actually went on to be bought by the public is another matter) and 11,500 to book clubs in a month, making more than 45,000 copies in less than three months: hardly failed magic and particularly impressive when one remembers what a dreary jacket Secker & Warburg gave it, and that it was listed in the *Spectator* as one of the worst books of the year.

The magic again also fell on the runners-up: Malcolm Bradbury's *Rates of Exchange* sold 3,480 copies in the months before its name reached the Booker short-list and 8,948 thereafter, whilst Graham Swift's *Waterland* sold 10,000 after joining the short-list of potential winners. Sales of Salman Rushdie's *Shame* were even greater than those of his prize-winning *Midnight's Children*.

The Booker Prize does not just benefit one book or one author or publisher. In the year of Keneally, William Boyd's *An Ice-Cream War* and Timothy Mo's *Sour Sweet* sold well into five figures. As Timothy Mo said himself, 'The Booker gave me the sort of attention I could have worked another ten years to achieve. It made people open up my book and say yes, he is a good writer.' Moreover, the whole shenanigans gets people into bookshops, widens their range of reading, encourages them to sample new young authors and suggests books as presents rather than records, tapes, jerseys or chocolates. Betting on books through bookies may shock the literati but getting three million people to watch a book programme on the television and arguing about it afterwards is an achievement not to be sneezed at.

In 1983 forty-one publishers submitted novels for the Booker Prize, which shows that fiction is in a very lively state. Novels came from such small publishers as Daedalus, Prosperity Publications, Virtuoso Books, the St Pancras Press and Sheba as well as the better-known fiction houses. Such has been the success engendered by the Booker that others have been encouraged to promote prizes. Whitbread's award £3,000 each to best biography, best novel and best children's novel; encouraged by all the publicity, a couple of years ago Whitbread's offered an extra prize, worth £2,000, for the best first novel, to be decided by the votes of a dozen unpaid literary editors. This open contest to encourage young writers, the unusual and the bizarre, has given a boost to the smaller publisher and has been hailed as the baby Booker. Most recently they have added a £1,000 prize for the best short story by a young writer.

There have been many criticisms levelled at the Booker Prize: it has been said to boost non-books, that it is unfair for publishers to have to make a pre-selection of four novels from their annual list, that some publishers submit more than their share, that the sole beneficiaries are a handful of rapacious publishers and their lucky authors, that it encourages seedy mediocrity and debases true literature but as Bernard Levin has pointed out, 'Neither Harold Robbins nor Marghanita Laski, neither the books business nor the lofty idealist, have any power to harm or to create literature, which has never been, cannot be, and never will be created by anything but the interaction of a single mind and a single soul.'

I once promoted a poetry competition myself, backed by a rich American patron of my acquaintance and judged by Sir

John Betjeman, Stevie Smith and Brian Patten. I hired a girl to sort through the 63,000 entries and put her in a room in Islington with a big wastepaper basket. After three months she had found only seventeen poems she considered worthy of publication. The wife of my rich patron fell into a terrible rage and demanded to see the rejects – then had to agree. The winner was a schoolgirl, whose first line read, 'I'm alright mother, but what about you?'

I arranged for the prizes to be presented at Burton Constable, the most famous recusant house in England, after a mayoral reception at Hull. (On the train Sir John suddenly announced, 'We must be near Ely.' 'Why?' I inquired. 'Because of the noise the wheels are making. We are riding on a bed of reeds.') To celebrate the occasion I wanted an eagle to swoop down on the judges as they swept up the drive in their horse-drawn carriage. Eagles, I knew, do not fly for fun, the weight of their wings makes it too like hard work. 'Don't worry,' said the trainer, 'I'll starve him for five days and he'll swoop all right.' But it wasn't all right on the day. The eagle never landed.

When I asked the headmistress if the winner might come to the prize-giving there had been a long silence down the telephone, then a grudgingly given assent. 'You don't sound very pleased.' 'We've just had to expel her.' She appeared, a magnificent sight in glossy boots and striking gear: a winner in all senses of the word.

Most of the poems were smug, cosy, complacent, reminding me of bad Patience Strong. Why? That's England for you. At about the same time Holt Rinehart had run a similar competition to mine in Chicago, just after the riots. The results were outstanding.

Perhaps we should try one in Belfast . . .

# XIV *Book fairs*

There are many book fairs during the year throughout the world, small, large, local, foreign, for antiquarians, for children's books, for booksellers and for publishers, but there is only one Frankfurt.

Before the war the International Book Fair's venue was Leipzig and reflected the elegance, charm and leisureliness of that city, since destroyed by Allied bombardment. Frankfurt is the incarnation of German *Wirtschaftswunder*. Being the centre of the American Zone it acquired a big airport, then hotels, then a conference and exhibition centre, bigger and uglier than anything in the world. In 1983 – the 35th Book Fair – 300,000 titles were exhibited, there were 900 new publishers, 2,300 new visitors, which makes for heavy party-going and adultery. There are nine halls with twenty-six aisles from A to Z, each a hundred yards long. It is purely a publishers' fair, sans booksellers, sans authors but very much *with* remainder merchants, hovering like vultures waiting for the newborn titles to die of under-exposure.

Almost every publisher mentioned in this book was there, in three minutes' stroll one could bump into Robin Denniston, donnish and dishevelled, George Weidenfeld, Sonny Mehta, Peter Israel and André Deutsch, who had just lost the new Norman Mailer when the auction passed £80,000.

The atmosphere is very democratic. The supremos of the publishing world sit bunched in their booths and are easily bearded. They are without their retinue, which is busy trying to sell books to the grim lady from the Steimatzky chain of booksellers in Israel, where a title with sales over sixteen copies is a bestseller.

Each Frankfurt is marked by an event. One year it was decided to honour Sir Victor Gollancz with an international award and in his speech of acknowledgment he chose the theme of forgiveness and opined that he was sure that God had forgiven Hitler. This year – 1983 – the event was less spectacular. The scream of police sirens barely penetrated our Hall but the increased hubbub from Hall 5 was perceptible: 'what was going on?' people asked each other. Answer, eventually, a group of Iranians was attacking the Iraqi stand, vice-versa, or was it Iranians *v.* Iranians? (Yes.) No matter, it was somewhere over there near the Scandinavian section.

Throughout the year in editorial meetings in publishing houses (q.v. Weidenfeld) it has been said, 'Well, let's get a dummy and show it at Frankfurt.' Publishers' stands, incidentally, are uniformly modest, so that Christopher Hurst's (q.v.) would be the same size as that of IPC's; he, with two employees including himself, and they, with thousands, display their current wares and past successes more as indicators of the style of book they publish than for sale at the Fair. If the books are any good the foreign rights will already have been sold but obviously Faber & Faber are going to display all of their Nobel Prize-winning author William Golding's titles even if all rights are already sold. The real business is done from 'dummies'. A dummy is often only a blank book with a cobbled-together jacket, the ultimate in 'try on', but it sometimes works. In the mounting hysteria of the Fair a publisher who returns to base without having bought anything can feel emasculated – a foolish fellow. He should remember Walter Harrap's advice, 'Let's take a risk and turn it down.'

Here is a story of Frankfurt at its best, meaning the place where a book can be sold on sight, something which could not happen anywhere else. We – the publishers 'we', meaning I – persuaded an artist called June Burnett, an octoroon lady from Stoke-on-Trent, at the sight of whose face (she says) children scream (until they sense her magic gentleness), to draw Adam delighting in God's creatures for the first time. So she drew the first ladybird crawling up Adam's thumb and Adam holding the first thrush in his hands; the result was absolutely charming.

I had flown in with the drawings on Sunday morning. The artist, who had been staying with me in London, had captioned them from Genesis the night before, in her own hand. The book, which we thought could be called *Let There be Light*, was a natural for an international deal in that the colour separations could be done in Florence, the printing in Yugoslavia and the 'black' (drawn from Genesis in the vernacular) supplied on film to the printers. Most publishing houses possess a Bible . . .

Our rights lady had an appointment with the Swedish publishers Norstedt, intending to sell them the rights to *Super-Ted*. On the off-chance she took the drawings of *Let There be Light* and returned to our stand in high spirits with an order for 4,000 copies.

Frankfurt always rates a piece in the posh papers. In one article a journalist commented, '80 per cent of the deals struck at the Fair are reneged upon.' One wonders how he arrived at this calculation. Did he have evidence before him of one hundred deals of which eighty had not subsequently been ratified (percentage talk is the bane of the twentieth century)? Or had he heard of five deals, four of which did not come off and applied with his calculator – another bane – a multiplying factor?

No, it is more likely that he had been boozing in the Frankfurterhof with a becalmed publisher from the stand next to Jonathan Cape's, where Tom Maschler was besieged by foreign publishers bidding for Dr Jonathan Miller's pop-up book on genitalia. Publishers rarely take revenge, just as they rarely cheat on royalties. If there is honour among thieves then there has to be honour in our profession too.

Book fairs are places where cross-pollination takes place, where deals are done, enemies made, new friends found and where the spin-off can be startling. It's not what takes place in the hothouse atmosphere of a fair that counts, it's what follows later that is important. After one such fair, I went big game hunting.

Anaheim, south of Los Angeles, is not a pretty spot; it is the site of Disneyland, an extravaganza which reeks of capitalist morality and milkshakes. It is also a conference centre, and thither repaired in 1982 3,000-odd members of the American Booksellers Association to be wooed by American publishers who set up showy stands. There are also hangers-on, in the shape of British publishers, remainder merchants, New Zealanders, Hungarians and Professor Brown of Florida University who had taken a stand to display his privately published book on farts. Having bought the British rights to this title, which includes an unpublished harangue from Benjamin Franklin on the subject to the *Académie Française* (to redress a snub), I felt free to accept an invitation to dinner from Conrad Goulden (see Book Clubs) in his elegant suite at a hotel in more salubrious Los Angeles.

Accompanied by my wife, a young lady who, to paraphrase Proust, had not seen the hawthorn flower that many times, we dined with Sam Marks, an octogenarian executive from MGM who had discovered Elizabeth Taylor and who, by dint of keeping his head down throughout the many executions at the studio, had survived as archivist.

He invited my wife to lunch at the lot and, as my date for that day had reneged, I was able to horn in on the invitation, an appropriate expression since the film we were treated to before lunch was hardish-core pornography from Brazil. It was clear, as one embarrassed MGM executive after another left the viewing theatre, that there had been some mistake. This, it was explained, was because MGM had wanted to screentest a Brazilian actress for a role in a major movie (are there any major movies?) and they wanted to see her at work, if that is the right word. Sam was deeply embarrassed and repeatedly pointed out to Laura that she was not obliged to sit it out through politeness; but we did, right through to the squelchy climax. After lunch in the canteen, a democratic affair since Sam Goldwyn's suite had been long subsumed, we went to Sam's office where he handed me an elderly copy of a typescript stamped 'copyright MGM July 14th, 1945', entitled *The Tenth Man* by Graham Greene.

Graham Greene, like Scott Fitzgerald and other writers before him, had been hired by the studio to write stories which might become movies. He had stayed at the Bel-Air Hotel and been paid fifteen hundred dollars a month. *All* copyright throughout the world in what he wrote under this deal belonged to his employers.

I read the novella that night and telephoned Sam in the morning. 'I thought you might be interested,' he remarked mildly.

*The Tenth Man* is set in a provincial town in France just occupied by the Germans. Among a group of hostages is a successful lawyer in his forties and a bitter young man in his twenties. When the lawyer draws a short straw and is one of the ten chosen to be shot in reprisal for the assassination of a German officer, he successfully barters his worldly goods for the life of the bitter young man. This arrangement is honoured by both sides; the young man is duly executed and so are documents transferring the lawyer's house, his practice and his bank balance to the younger man's sister and mother. After the war when he is released, the lawyer, destitute and suspect, tramps Paris in search of a job. The atmosphere of that city, derelict, frightened and, again, suspicious, is, as the reviewers will say – if they get the chance – splendidly evoked. Our hero hoofs it home and, disguised, persuades the invalid mistress of the house to employ him as an odd-job man. He is strangely familiar with his surroundings and there are some breathtaking moments when he might be detected. He falls in love with the daughter. He is eventually denounced as an impostor by a travelling circus performer, himself an impostor. He is betrayed by a fellow resistance worker who thinks he has betrayed *him*. The local priest enters the act as often in France and *always* in Graham Greene. There is blood all over the floor. Splendid, vintage stuff. First print 20,000 hardcover. Obvious big paperback sale. Share (unbelievable!) of foreign rights. Just one of Greene's publishers, Laffont, never prints less than 40,000. Giddy dreams for a publisher who has just bought back his own imprint and could use a coup.

Antony White, my partner, negotiated a contract with MGM's lawyer for a reasonable advance and provision of 6 per cent of the royalties for the maestro to dispose of as he wished. There was no doubt that MGM had all rights in this property but it seemed prudent and good-mannered to check it out.

I put my finger to the wind.

Max Reinhardt of The Bodley Head, Graham Greene's usual British publisher and normally imperturbable, perturbed: 'You are treading in a minefield my boy,' he hissed to me when we bumped into each other on the staircase at Joe Allen's, a Bohemian dungeon frequented by glitterati and wealthy TV cameramen. He is right, Graham Greene is a literary monument and does not like his foundation disturbed, nor early work, of which there is much and with which he is not always satisfied. Furthermore, though the title to publish in America was clear, his assignment and copyright to MGM under the terms of his contract in 1945 might have been vitiated or certainly muddied by a British Act of Parliament in 1956, or so my partner's lawyer implied in a masterly analysis, of a clarity beyond the capacity of most American lawyers.

So there, in a barely animate state, the matter rested, until one evening in New York, Robert Mayall, the PR man for (amongst other enterprises) Mitsubishi, invited me to spend a few days in the South of France with his father-in-law, who had a comfortable estate just above Nice, in the hills. 'Near Antibes,' I mused, where, I knew from cross letters to *The Times*, that my quarry lived. Robert's wife Jennifer is an Oxford friend of my wife Laura which is how we met. Apart from both having pretty young wives we have nothing in common. He is an ex-Nam Colonel, right-wing wasp and teetotal. And I am . . . well, different. But we enjoyed our differences. We could block out, together in the Provençal sunshine by the pool, a proposal for his exposé of the public relations game, tentatively entitled *The Mind-Fuckers*, and I could pursue *The Tenth Man*.

Lady Celestria Noel is a literary lady with a sharp pen whose reader's reports are held in esteem by the publishing fraternity. She is also a Catholic noblewoman of impeccable pedigree – her mother is a Stourton – and she agreed to be my travelling companion. We set off on a reconnaissance trip from La Forestière du Loup, our host's domain, in one of his many cars, and our first stop was to take a drink off *my* former father-in-law, John Strachey, a contemporary of Graham Greene's who also lived in Antibes and would surely know the habits of our prey. We already knew his address.

Strachey knew more than that; he knew the former Gibraltar policeman who was Graham Greene's unofficial bodyguard protecting the master from people like me. He lived in the same apartment building and was in the telephone book. I was urged to call him up and fortified by a pastis I did so. There was no reply.

Well, Graham Greene lunched every day at Felix au Port and there Lady Celestria and I went, arriving at 2 o'clock. The restaurant was nearly empty and certainly Greeneless. I had been reading the latest book about our author, a series of interviews by a French lady journalist. The back cover bore a picture of Mr Greene, a bad likeness as I was later to discover. I laid it on the table as I paid the bill, adding a discernible tip. It was easy to engage the proprietor in conversation about the habits of his most distinguished customer who, he told me, turned up every day just before *midi*, nearly always lunched alone and only consumed one *plat*. We decided to return the next day to coincide with his arrival and though we couldn't perhaps manage a meal at that hour we could always do justice to a bottle of champagne . . .

That night I had a nightmare. In his youth Graham Greene, who has all his life been attracted by danger, used to play Russian Roulette. In my dream he had said to me, 'Yes you can publish my book but first let's play this game.' I woke up just as I was pressing the trigger. Swiftly I rewrote the final scene in my waking mind. The revolver had gone off, killing me, and Graham Greene had been excoriated for causing the death of a publisher in the prime of an interesting career. (Some reactions to the proposed publication of *The Tenth Man* had been that it would be shameful to exploit the reputation of a great man by publishing a work of his of which he did not approve.)

The next day Celestria and I arrived chez Felix at about twenty past twelve. It was pretty hot but we insisted on sitting inside at a table next to a man I supposed to be Graham Greene. I didn't recognize him until I noticed the slightly bulbous eyes I had read about. He had been talking in French, with an accent which owed more to Berkhamsted than Biarritz, to the only other occupant of the restaurant, but when he saw us approach he retreated into contemplation of a sort of posh glossy and into the consumption of what could have been a *blanquette de veau*. Celestria sat opposite me looking at Graham Greene, I parallel to him a few feet away, never looking at him. I already felt some of that fear and doubt which must shake the resolution of a hunter when the game he has been stalking appears framed nobly in his sights. I don't remember how the next hour passed but Celestria and I rattled away, exchanging anecdotes which grew in vivacity and colour as the champagne bottle emptied. Then, in mid-flow, Graham Greene left – it seemed to me without paying the bill. Perhaps he had some arrangement with the proprietor? But he came back and ordered an icecream.

He appeared to take absolutely no notice of my assault on his attention though I was aware, until I stopped noticing anything, that he had not turned the page of his magazine. Then suddenly he was not there. So intoxicated by the exuberance of my own verbosity and three-quarters of a bottle of champagne had I been, that I had not registered his departure.

In the fly-leaf of the book I had been carrying I had written in shaky pencil, 'For Anthony Blond. I see no reason why *The Tenth Man* should not be published.' It looked as if this bow at a venture would never be deployed, until Monsieur Felix spotted our distress. Thinking us Graham Greene fans hoping for his signature, he picked up the book and cried out, 'But Monsieur has not signed!' 'I did not like to embarrass him,' I replied (may God forgive me). 'Never mind,' said Monsieur Felix, 'he will sign it for me, he is not only a customer, he is a friend,' and he hurried out of his restaurant in pursuit of the maestro.

(A beat, as they say in the movie business.) I dared not look round, Celestria provided a running commentary. 'He's caught up with him, he's stopped, he's looking at the book, he's got out his spectacles . . . He's got out *another* pair of spectacles, he's reading it, he's got out his pen, he's writing something . . .' Monsieur Felix hurried back into the restaurant. 'Monsieur a signé.' He had indeed. Under the clear and legible message 'I see every reason,' was the equally clear and legible signature 'Graham Greene'.

'Hard luck Blond,' said Celestria. 'No,' said I, 'First round.' We sped to a flower shop and bought an armful of tiger-lilies. We discussed the nature of the message on the card. 'Just put "Well done",' said Celestria, with the authority of a thousand years of social security behind her.

The correspondence that ensued was fulsome on my part, cryptic (via his sister in Crowborough, Sussex) on his. *The Tenth Man* was written, he complained, under 'a slave contract' when he was in a state of economic distress. No, he couldn't be bothered to write a preface saying why the book shouldn't be published – which we would then publish. His tone was always courteous, however, and in one letter he even agreed to read my own novel which I sent him, provided he broke a leg or something and had a long convalescence. His last letter, however, seemed final since he said that he had asked his regular publisher, Max Reinhardt of The Bodley Head (to which house he had moved after a public tiff with Heinemann over the manner in which they had let go Mr Frere, their Managing Director), to repay me my expenses in the matter.

Max Reinhardt gave me lunch at Rules. After half an hour of statutory gossip he announced, 'Graham wants to do it.' On the back of the menu we wrote out the deal: *THE TENTH MAN to be published jointly by B H and A B with equal billing, our contract with M G M* (over whose validity in the UK there was a smidgen of doubt) *to be subsumed by a new contract between B H and A B and G G giving him a larger royalty and the lion's share of foreign rights*. No agent was involved (tee hee). A few weeks later Graham Greene sent the revised typescript with an introduction and appropriate reminiscence and Max Reinhardt flew off with it to Simon & Schuster in New York. The deal was acceptable to us because it involved no fuss, and surely a slice of fruit cake is better than the whole of a penny bun.

Back on the MGM lot the studio doves were fluttering. How could they have parted with a potential bestseller for so little money? Sam Marks, the archivist, who has now left the organization, pointed out that a) they didn't know that they owned it, and b) that having paid Graham Greene $1,000 a week for ten weeks nearly forty years ago – such a slave contract it wasn't. They would probably make a profit in the end, not to speak of making a film.

*The Tenth Man* was published by The Bodley Head in association with Anthony Blond in spring 1985.

The print order was 40,000 copies.

# *Envoi*

If, at the end of reading this book, you feel that you might like to enter the publishing profession yourself, then re-read Ed Victor's account of how he started on pp. 26–30 and also John Brown's on pp. 38–41. Find out which publishers are advertising for staff in the *Bookseller*, write them a letter, mentioning with enthusiasm their most recent successful book, and offer to do anything and everything for the firm you have chosen.

A winning letter of application for a job in publishing (suggested in *The Publishing Game*) has been copied and used so much over the last ten years that editors are tired of receiving it. I therefore suggest that you invent your own letter conveying:

That publishing is the passion of your life
That you have worked in a bookshop, on a magazine or in some bookish sphere
That you admire their particular house because . . .
That you number many potential writers among your friends and contemporaries.

Expect to find a publisher's office somewhat bizarre. None is typical so I shall end this book by describing mine. We work in rooms dotted around two linked, originally seventeenth-century houses where we moved in 1984, not a mashie shot from Gray's Inn. We occupy about half the space, of which we own the freehold. The basement is dedicated to elderly files which no one has dared to disturb and boasts a telex machine. A sort of extended potting shed in the garden houses the trade counter, despatch and photocopier and is dominated by *Sandy* (the 'Duchess'), also in charge of the 'gofer', sometimes a young man anxious to get into publishing or a relation anxious not to.

Adjacent, on the ground floor, is the bower of *Hilary*, in charge of rights and contracts who, on grounds of seniority and inability to panic, is the Deputy Managing Director.

Above her on the next floor sits *Sally*, who controls the accounts assisted by an asthmatic computer. On the same level in the next building – the multiplicity of doors sometimes creates a Feydeau-like atmosphere – *Peter* masterminds production and *Hal* the editorial dept, assisted by *Hayley*.

Back in the other house on the second floor *Sarah* looks after publicity, occasionally assisted by *Laura*, who once got the Royal Engineers to agree to build a Bailey Bridge over the Street of Shame. (It wasn't allowed.) Next door, which doubles as a conference room, sits Sarah's sister *Clare* sorting out and reporting on the 'slush pile' – the unsolicited manuscripts which are, *terrible dictu* the publishers' peculiar bane.

The *piano nobile*, if one can say that, is a double, white-panelled room with six windows down to the ground and a long, Regency table covered with baize, appropriate matching chairs where sit my partner and myself and, theoretically, a fire blazing at either end and a corner cupboard with decanters of sherry. There is just room for the desks of *Joanna*, the publishing manager, who liaises with Century (to whom our sales are sub-contracted) and with the warehouse (ditto) in Tiptree, Essex. Our not always trivial rounds and common tasks are controlled by *Anna* – another desk – whose first and, we pray, last employment this is.

Our company publishes about forty titles a year, varying from an adventure of *SuperTed* at 75p to the *Encyclopedia of Naive Art* at £47.50. Currently our turnover is a million plus and we expect profits of around 10 per cent.

We are quite happy
thank you very much

*London, August Bank Holiday 1984*

# *Bibliography*

There is no shortage of books about books, but for the trivial rounds of publishing and for job-hunting read the *Bookseller*, published by the enormously rich family firm of Whitakers of 12 Dyott Street, WC1, and *Publishing News*, owned by the much less rich but amiable Clive Labovitch and Fred Newman of 43 Museum Street, WC1. They also publish the best middle-brow magazine of reviews, *Books and Bookmen*. For higher brows there is *The Times Literary Supplement*, *The Literary Review* (owned by Naim Attallah q.v.) and *The London Review of Books*, sister to the prestigious and boring *New York Review of Books*. The National Book League has a catalogue called *Books about Books* and the man who runs the show, the ubiquitous and mellifluous Martyn Goff, has made the following selection.

## *Publishing: current practice*

*Books On Line: Proceedings of a Conference Organised by the Working Party of Libraries and the Book Trade at Book House on 12th May 1981*, LIBTRAD 1981. Top representatives from the worlds of bookselling, publishing and librarianship discuss computer technology as it will affect the book trade.

Priscilla Oakeshott and Clive Bradley (editors), *The Future of the Book: Part 1 – The impact of New Technologies: a Report*

*prepared by the Publishers Association* (Unesco, 1982)
Fourteen specialists consider the nature and likely impact of new technology trends on traditional forms of publishing, bookselling and reading.

Audrey and Philip Ward, *The Small Publisher: a Manual and Case Histories* (Oleander Press, 1979)
A guide to the running of a small publishing business in the 1980s.

## *History and biography*

Michael S. Howard, *Jonathan Cape, Publisher* (Cape, 1971)
An account of the fifty years' history of the firm with much literary anecdote.

Ian Norrie, *Mumby's Publishing and Bookselling in the Twentieth Century* 6th ed. (Bell & Hyman, 1982)
Supplements *Publishing and Bookselling*.

Sir Stanley Unwin, *The Truth about Publishing* 8th ed. (Allen & Unwin, 1976)
Since it was first published in 1926, this book has been translated into at least a dozen languages and is still the standard textbook on publishing, now revised by Philip Unwin.

## *Bookselling: current practice*

Irene Babbidge, *Beginning in Bookselling* (Deutsch/Gower Publishing, revised edition 1972)
A much-used handbook for those starting in bookselling, covering all aspects of bookshop practice.

Sydney Hyde (editor), *Selling the Book: a Bookshop Promotion Manual* (Bingley, 1977)
A topical collection of short contributions by well-known book-trade people covering continental practice, book clubs, display, local community liaison, etc.

## *Reading and bookbuying*

Euromonitor, *The Book Report (incorporating the Euromonitor Book Readership Survey)* (Euromonitor Publications annual paperback 108.00)
Extremely useful survey material, especially on readership statistics.

## *Also recommended*

Richard Findlater (editor), *Author! Author!* (Faber & Faber, 1984)
A selection from the journal of the Society of Authors. It includes a pleasantly bad-tempered exchange of views between Arnold Bennett and H. G. Wells on the value or otherwise of literary agents.

J. Hepburn, *The Author's Empty Purse and the Rise of the Literary Agent* (Oxford University Press, 1969)

Publishers feature as characters in many novels, notably in *The Way of All Flesh* by Samuel Butler and Grant Richards in *Nicholas Crabbe* by Fr Rolfe.
Readers seeking portraits of this author/publisher are directed to *The Partners* by Desmond Briggs (Secker & Warburg), *The Face of the Waters* by Simon Raven, *The Blackmailer* by Isabel Colegate and *Fathers and Lovers* by Cressida Lindsay.

# *Glossary*

ABA
The conference of the American Booksellers Association. Annually, e.g. at Anaheim, Dallas, San Francisco – second only to Frankfurt as a publishers' draw.

advance
Sum paid by publishers to authors by publication on account of royalties which it is hoped will be earned.

Art paper (US coated paper)
Glossy paper suitable for the reproduction of illustrations in a book.

B.A.
Booksellers Association.

bestseller
No strict usage.

bleed
An illustration that goes right to the edge of the page.

blurb
Publishers' description and (over) estimation of a book. Usually printed on the inside flaps of the jacket. *Fr.* Blah Blah, *Sp.* Bombo.

block (US engravings)
Mechanically or chemically engraved metal plate used in the letterpress process for reproducing line or halftone illustrations.

blues/ozalids
Photocopies of the text and/or pictures of a book, usually provided for a final check before printing.

bodice ripper
Sexy novels in historical disguise.

boss copy
Authoritative copy, e.g. Victor Gollancz's advertisements.

bulk
Technically the width of the book without the binding, but often used as a transitive verb meaning to bulk out a thin book by using heavier paper and make it appear more substantial than the text alone allows.

cadet edition
The rude words taken out for children, e.g. *The Cruel Sea.*

colophon
A publisher's symbol, originally printed on the last page, now usually on the title page and jacket.

copyright
The exclusive right of an author to produce his own work and protection against plagiarism of every signatory of the Berne Convention (1956).

cosy
An invention of Desmond Elliot's to describe a rural anodyne saga.

dissing
To break up type no longer needed for a reprint of a letterpress book (becoming *Arch.*)

erratum slip
A last-minute correction to the text of a book after it has been two-thirds printed, usually stuck in.

(I)SBN
(International) Standard Book Number. Publishers started assigning such numbers from 1967 (not mandatory) each made up of ten digits broken into four groups. Group 1 identifies the country (e.g. 0 = English language speaking countries), Group 2 identifies the publisher (anything from 2 to 7 digits), Group 3 identifies the book and Group 4 is the checking figure (single digit) you need to add to the total after each digit has been multiplied successively with its predecessor and all the results added together to make the whole sequence divisible by eleven!

letterpress
Printing from raised characters, the oldest method of printing.

litho (graphy)
Printing from smooth plate or cylinder.

lively author
An author who is constantly on the telephone.

logo
US for colophon.

machine (*vb*)
The action of printing by letterpress or by lithography.

net
The price of a book in a bookshop is a net price below which the bookseller may not sell without permission. At great expense the P.A. convinced the Restrictive Practices Court that books should be exempt from the conditions of the 1964 Act on retail price maintenance.

non-book
Scornful description of a publication designed to appeal to those who regard a book as an object to look at rather than to read.

non-net
Technically the opposite of net. In fact applies only to books sold to institutions like schools through educational contractors. The whole structure of discounts between net and non-net is different.

one-off
A 'one-off' author or a 'one-off' book means that the publisher thinks the author has only one book in him, or that he has borrowed the author from another publisher for a specific series.

outright
Articles for symposia, or even whole books, can be bought outright by a publisher, i.e. with no royalty payments.

override
A percentage offered to a hardback publisher by a paperback company who control volume rights in a title.

P.A.
Publishers Association.

package
A book conceived, controlled and printed by a packager (q.v.).

'perfect binding'
A method of binding a book with hot glue on to guillotined sheets, i.e. not sewing and therefore often imperfect.

perfect number
When a book can be printed and bound in sections of 32 pages, i.e. most economically.

permission
Fee payable by publishers wishing to reprint passages in excess of 'fair dealing' (see pages 99–100). Music is particularly expensive and tricky.

PLR
Public Lending Right. A system of rewarding authors from public library issues of their works. Described by Mr Carter, who drafted the UK legislation, as 'phoney, ill-considered, unworkable and a significant misapplication of public money'.

prelims
The pages before the main text of a book, often given roman numerals.

public domain
Anything in print fifty years after the author's death, or after posthumous first publication, is not in copyright.

pulp (*vb*)
Books, usually paperbacks, which it is impossible to remainder or dump are 'pulped' and new paper made of them.

pulp fiction (*n.*)
Cheap novels.

reader's report
An opinion of the worth of a manuscript submitted to a publisher. Writing them is a minor art and poorly paid.

remainders
The rump of unsaleable stock is bought by remainder merchants for a humiliating price. They give good parties.

reverting rights
If a book goes out of print or the publisher goes bust, the author or agent will ask for copyright back.

river of white
Accidental optical effect caused by vertical juxtaposition of spaces between words.

royalties
Percentage of the published price of a book payable to the author.

separate
'We're separating in Zagreb' means the publishers have decided to use cheaper, Yugoslav processors for separating the colours of the illustrations for an art book.

setting
Sometimes called composing. The act of a printer who transcribes a typescript on to a machine.

sheet deal
Sale of flat or folded collated sheets of an edition to another (US) publisher or library contractor.

sight unseen
A book so formidable that it can be bought by a publisher blindly, e.g. Peter Israel of Putnams USA offered $3.5m to Yoko Ono for her memoirs.

slaver
Books describing the trade in black-flesh for sado-masochists.

softcover or paperback
A book printed on a rotary machine, with a soft paper cover.

step up
A soft/hard publishing deal linked to a likely film – see override.

stroke
'We can stroke in Bombay' means cheap nimble Indian fingers key stroke the composition on a sophisticated computer.

subscription
The number of copies ordered by booksellers prior to publication.

take over
Slightly scornful description by paperback companies when US books are bought by hardback publishers or vice versa.

teasers
Small ads in trade magazines designed to intrigue.

wash top (US 'stained')
Colouring the top of a book to make it look prettier.

widow
Single word at the end, top or bottom of a page.
Thus

# *Useful and boring information*

Every trade has its own institutions and mags; here are some in publishing.

*The Publishers Association*
19 Bedford Square, WC1
Is what it says. Lobbies for publishers up to Cabinet level, e.g. VAT. Members often think of resigning but if they do the current Chief Executive, Clive Bradley, is coaxy enough to woo them back, e.g. Paul Hamlyn. They beaver away in a handsome house in prime Bloomsbury.

*The Booksellers Association*
154 Buckingham Palace Road, SW11
Ditto for booksellers but in a depressing building. They do their best, e.g. the Charter group.

*P.E.N. International*
A worthy, up-market lot who hold conferences in Balkan cities with unpronounceable names, with the admirable intention of promoting 'writers in the lesser known languages'. The English bit is run by Francis King from 7 Dilke Street, SW3. The American end by surprisingly, Norman Mailer.

*The Society of Authors*
84 Drayton Gardens, SW10
The oldest protagonist for authors recently revitalized. Man-

age dead authors' estates and will help a live one if the case is 'sound in ethics and law'.

*The Writers' Guild of Great Britain*
430 Edgware Road, W2
Was lively and leftish under the late John Gould. Big in promoting PLR and the claims of TV scripters.

*The Bookseller*
14 Dyott Street, WC1
*The* weekly parish mag of the trade. A must for job hunters and contains all the logistics and statistics and the odd mild joke. Edited by Louis Baum, a rather special South African.

*Publishing News*
43 Museum Street, WC1
The tabloid of the trade; paperback and palace coup oriented. Clive Labovitch, gregarious and accident prone, also co-owns *Books and Bookmen* which has pieces on publishing.

*PIMS*
4 St John's Place, EC1
An expensive and invaluable monthly guide to the media and to those who run around within them.

*National Book League*
45 East Hill, Wandsworth, SW18
Establishment organization run by galvanic Martyn Goff.

There are a number of highbrow journals which review books in some depth and fervour, notably *The Times Literary Supplement*, *Encounter*, *The London Review of Books*, *The Literary Review*, *The London Magazine* and (with wit) *The Spectator*.

*The Groucho* (not boring)
A new club (1985) designed by trendy Tchaik Chassay where we all hang out.

# *Index*

## Index

# Index